YoungWriters

Past Poets - Future Voices

2010 Poetry Competition for 11-18 year-olds

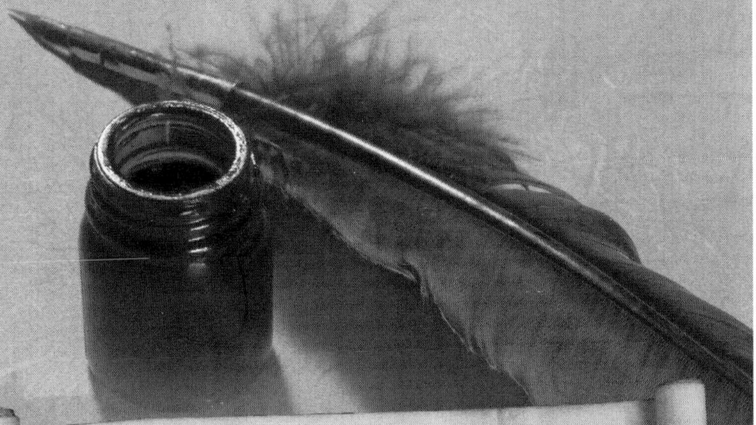

Expressions From The UK

Edited by Amy Brownlie & Mark Richardson

First published in Great Britain in 2010 by

 Young**Writers**

Remus House
Coltsfoot Drive
Peterborough
PE2 9JX
Telephone: 01733 890066
Website: www.youngwriters.co.uk

All Rights Reserved
Book Design by Ali Smith & Tim Christian
© Copyright Contributors 2010
SB ISBN 978-0-85739-166-7

Foreword

Young Writers was established in order to promote creativity and a love of reading and writing in children and young adults. We believe that by offering them a chance to see their own work in print, their confidence will grow and they will be encouraged to become the poets of tomorrow.

Our latest competition 'Past Poets - Future Voices' was specifically designed as a showcase for secondary school pupils, giving them a platform with which to express their ideas, aspirations and passions. In order to expand their skills, entrants were encouraged to use different forms, styles and techniques.

Selecting the poems for publication was a difficult yet rewarding task and we are proud to present the resulting anthology. We hope you agree that this collection is an excellent insight into the voices of the future.

Contents

Jade Llewellyn (14) 1
Joe Rose (12) 2

Bishop Milner Catholic School, Dudley
Connor Redding (12) 2
Franco Giovenco (12) 3
Kiaran Marsh (11) 4
Nerissa Chater (12) 5
Daniel Platt (12) 6
Matthew Holland (11) 7
Munashe Muchena (13) 8
Lydia Humphreys (13) 9
Daniel James (12) 10
Kym Fitzpatrick (13) 11

Cardinal Griffin Catholic High School, Cannock
Hannah Dutton (12) 12
Danielle Austin (13) 13
Victoria Hampton (13) 14
Zac Stanley (13) 15
Sophie Fletcher (13) 16
Hannah Hale (13) 17
Ariana Foley (13) 18
Nikita Del-Giudice (13) 19
Faye Louise Harvey (13) 20
Shannon Collins (13) 21
Abby Marie Liddington (13) 21
Polly Smith (12) 22
Ben Chamberlin (13) 22
Connor Butcher (13) 23
Michael Rose (13) 24
Imogen Jones (11) 24
Sophie Palmer (13) 25
Natasha Woodall (12) 25
Shannon Malone (13) 26
Morgan Challinor (12) 26
Sam Hollingmode (13) 27
Luke Round (11) 27
Sofie Jones (13) 28

Emily Fellows (11) 28
Steven Edwards (12) 29
Courtney Targett (12) 29
Chantelle Gunner (13) 30
Danielle White (11) 30
Tamara Hillman (11) 31
Paul Brewster (11) &
Owen Wilkes (12) 31
Iiona Kilgallon (12) 32
James Roberts (12) 32
Kate Hawkins (12) 33
Ryan Di Cesare (12) 33
Monika Bednarczyk &
Lara Morris (13) 34
Edward Page (13) 34
Megan Walker (12) 35

Churnet View Middle School, Leek
Bethany Wood (13) 35
Ella Cope (13) 36
Robert Alexander (12) 37
Robert Salt (13) 38
Natalie Stacie Wilson (12) 39
Mischa Balderstone (13) 40
Rebecca Bennett (13) 41
Molly Belfield (13) 41

Hallmoor Special School, Birmingham
Alex Plumb (13) 42
Sean O'Brien (13) 42
Luke Roney (13) 42
Jordan Emerson (13) 42
Katherine Colbert (13) 43
Shaun Betts (13) 43
Haroon Ansar (13) 43

Haute Vallee School, Jersey
Daniel Managhan (11) 43

Chantalle Roberts (14) 44
Lisa Jaremyn (12) 44
Joe Birrell (14) 45
Daniel Robinson (14) 45
Nikita Binet (13) 46
Dominik Jagla (12) 46
Alex Langlois (13) 46
José Roberto Pestana (12) 47
Kevin Aubignac (12) 47
Alfie Ashpole (11) 47

Heronsbridge Special School, Bridgend
Josh Hamilton (15) 48

King Edward VI School, Stratford-upon-Avon
Nick Edmonds (15) 48

North Leamington School, Leamington Spa
Ellie Hickson (12) 49
Amy Biggs (11) 50
Sebastian Stuart (12) 51
Rachel Wells (11) 52
Charlie Jackson (11) 53
George Want (12) 54
Kyle Joyce (11) 55
Tom Harvey (12) 56
Daniela Cowell (11) 56
Jade Killingbeck (12) 57
Gregor Fletcher (11) 57
Isri Kaur Rai (12) 58
Emily Forman-Jessop (12) 58
Jessica Nash (12) 59
Lauren Cowlishaw (12) 60
Keris Jones (11) 60
Rebecca O'Connell (12) 61
Sebastian Anker-Ryan (12) 61

Penryn College, Penryn
Kia Mogg (14) 62
Daniel Hesketh (15) 63
Josh Amar (12) 63
Hayley Dawson (15) 64

Daniel Altenberg (12) 64
Rosie Blindell (12) 65
Thalia Richardson (12) 65
Amy Glover (12) 66
Katie Edwards (12) 66
Jessica Gabriel (12) 67
Olli Haughton (12) 67
Zoe Osmond (12) 67
Jake Joyce (12) 68
Jodie Hodges (12) 68
Katie Walton (11) 68
Rosie Louise McGurk (12) 69
Josh Sharp (12) 69
Matthieu Bethermin (12) 69
Jake Jones (12) 70
Tiegan Johns (12) 70
Wayland Drury (12) 70

Pontypridd High School, Pontypridd
George Sims-Slater (11) 70
Hannah Eleri Davies (12) 71
Farah Iqbal (12) 72
Cara Sorenti (13) 73
Jemma Reeves (12) 73
Scott Jenkins (14) 74
Mark Hooper (13) 74
Matthew William Morgan (13) 75
Matthew Rawlins (13) 75
Leah Emery (12) 76
Bronwyn Phillips-Griffiths (11) 76
Ffion Rowlands (13) 77
Kyle Allen (14) 77
Rachel Burrows (12) 78
Cora Nott (12) 78
Natasha Hill (14) 79
Dani Jones (13) 79
Chloe Hooper (12) 80
Ian Kelland (14) 80
Samantha Thomas (12) 81
Chloe Lee Willetts (13) 81
Hannah Lee (12) 82
Carter Langford (14) 82
Jessica Davies (14) 83

Thomas Morris (14) 83
Daniel William Jones (11) 84
Rhiannon Wattley (13) 84
Zac Byard (12) 85
Jennifer Bohen (12) 85
Hollie Jones (14) 86
Karly Samuel (14) 86
Holly Rebecca Simmons (12) 87
Carys Ashcroft (12) 87
Matthew Lacey (13) 88
Amy-Jane Davies (14) 88
James Hoey (13) 89
Rebecca Williams (13) 89
Rachael Parr (14) 90
Paige Pritchard (11) 90
Rhys Goodwin (12) 91
Thomas Ashton (14) 91
Luke Price (14) 92
Jarrod Evans (13) 92
Emily Pardoe (14) 93
Lucy Watts (14) 93
Kate Taylor (12) 93
Amy Bishop (13) 94
Mathieu Austin (14) 94
Teigan Jones (12) 94
Morgan Bowen (14) 95
Aimee Louise Morris (12) 95
Jake Barlow (12) 95

Poole High School, Poole

Hannah McCrory (13) 96
Ellie Parr (13) 97
Graham Rigler (14) 98
Lauren Nicolson (14) 99
Danni Peart (13) 100
Dann Cobb (14) 101
Stacey Ayling (14) 101
Liam Jerrett (14) 102
Rebecca Phillips (13) 102
Robert Smith (13) 103
Hollie Brunyee (13) 103
Ryan Stiggants (13) 104
William Clayton (14) 104
Fraser Moors (14) 105

Josh Kitching (13) 105
Zachary Beavan (14) 106

Redland Green School, Bristol

Amy Cooper (12) 106
Aelliey Kelly (13) 107
Max Heiberg-Gibbons (13) 108
Hannah Crook (11) 110
Isobel Pickering (11) 111
Barnaby Mather (13) 112
Annie Allen (11) 113
Elliot Sandammeer Brewer (12) 114
Sophie Back (11) 115
Rachel Perry-Watts (12) 116
Saskia Wootton-Cane (11) 117
Tallulah Clark (12) 118
Isaac Williams (12) 118
Cameron Merchant (13) 119
Alex Brindle (12) 119
Saffy Haigh (12) 120
Jemima Pike (11) 120
Helen Birch (11) 121
Douglas Best (11) 121
Basir Naz (13) 122

St David's College, Llandudno

Jake Jones (11) 122
Nick Roden (12) 123
Alexander Maguire (12) 123
Charlie Marshall (12) 124
Zuzanna Kawalek (12) 125
Douglas Seale (12) 126
Louie Forte (11) 126

St Sampson's High School, Guernsey

Joshua Ozanne (12) 127
Adele Le Gallez (14) 127
Louise Dorey (13) 128
Ashleigh Pitman (14) 128
Laura Kirkpatrick (14) 129
Leah Foss (12) 129

Bethany Nicholson (11) 130
Owen Hunt (12) 130

Westlands School, Sittingbourne
Sonia Emerson (12) 130

Woking High School, Woking
Georgina Jaggs (13) 131
Elvie Mathis (11) 132
Georgina Gray 133
Lauren Brown (14) 134
Corey Aslin (14) 134
Rebecca Brown (12) 135
Ella Porter (14) 135
Ashleigh Thatcher (12) 136
Emma Stone (14) 136
Katie-Lauren Lewsza (11) 137
Chloe Alexis (12) 137
Isabel Meyler (12) 138
William Berry (12) 138
Sara Hill (12) 139
Ayman Sinada (12) 139
Mia-Siân Worrall (12) 140
Vina Murad (12) 140
Josh Bowden (13) 141
Steph Hamill (13) 141
Hannah Jones (13) 142
Megan Calderwood (13) 142
Valli McAdam (11) 143
Jacob Parvin (14) 143
Jonathan Abraham (14) 144
Sophie Osborne (12) 144
Jordon Hattersley (12) 145
David Dennington (13) 145
Corinne Heggie (14) 146
Christopher Shah (12) 146
Phoebe Stanmore (12) 147
Connor Mitchell (14) 147
Jamie Banszky (12) 148
Maryam Hussain (13) 148
Jennifer Kirk (11) 149
Daniel Pearce (11) 149

Finley Sale (12) 150
Sophie Little (12) 150
Jennie Bew (12) 151
Raheem Yusif Hussain (12) 151
Nazmiye Raif (14) 152
Daisy Jones (11) 152
Jordan Hookins (12) 153
Elizabeth Nay (14) 153
Nadeem Hussain 153
Abigail Hookins (12) 154
Megan MacAlister (12) 154
Lewis Sines (11) 154
Chloe Marsh (14) 155
Ben Hooper (14) 155
Alice Curr 155
Ayesha Rasool (14) 155
Idrees Ifzal (14) 156
Gemma Hemus (14) 156

The Poems

Destiny And Fate

I belong with you
Whether it's right or wrong
Destiny will choose its course
It won't be that long
Till they decide
If it's meant to be
For you and me
To be side by side.

I'm a big believer in destiny and fate
Not everything is handed on your plate
You gotta fight for what's right
Then everything will be in sight, yeah
There's nothing too big or nothing too small
You will still stand very tall
'Cause everything's gonna be alright
And you and I hopefully might.

So please wait, give us a chance
We can make it, I am sure
Who else makes you feel this way?
Our love is so pure
We will stand together, forever
For the rest of time
We will have the best adventure
And discover the great climb.

Jade Llewellyn (14)

The Right Path

Fathers and sons have a special connection.
They are taught to lead and lead others into the right way of life.
From the beginning of their lives they began to grow,
To develop and to lead.
Fathers are always proud of their sons
Because they are always special
And they are the ones that will follow the family name
And pass it on from generation to generation.
The fathers help to send their sons in the correct direction.
The fathers do not tell you which way to go
But they pick you up when you fall.

Joe Rose (12)

I'm A Full-Blooded British Stereotype
(Based on 'Stereotype' by John Agard)

I'm a full-blooded British stereotype. See my football? Watch it go.

I'm a full-blooded British stereotype, you ask if I got a cuppa in me blood. You think I'm a fancy man, well you're wrong.

I'm a full-blooded British stereotype. You think I can play. How do you know?
Smash! Watch it go.

I'm a full-blooded British stereotype, you like fish and chips, well have a bit of salt. But I'm no multimillionaire. I'm a full-blooded British stereotype who is ginger but I'm no singer.

Connor Redding (12)
Bishop Milner Catholic School, Dudley

Damien's Blessing
(A poem written in the style of Imtiaz Dharker's 'Blessing' using characters from the text 'Millions' by Frank Cottrell-Boyce)

The skin is getting thinner by the minute,
There never is enough food.

Imagine the biggest meal,
But only a small amount of it,
In an empty hand
The voice of a kindly god.

Sometimes, the sudden rush of fortune.
That I see my mum again
Silver flutters in the air
People have found millions
They have found shining gold.
For the huts, a congregation: even man, woman,
Child without a mother
They are alone now.
They find a
Well, cold,
Clear water.

A child screaming
For the family to know,
Their eyes are polished by the food and water
Glittering eyes everywhere
It is a sign from God,
They have all been blessed.

Franco Giovenco (12)
Bishop Milner Catholic School, Dudley

Anthony's Blessing
(A poem written in the style of Imtiaz Dharker's 'Blessing' using characters from the text 'Millions' by Frank Cottrell-Boyce)

My eyes glow like a bulb
My dream is in front of me.

Imagine the smell of it
The first small spend
Of the millions
Which I have.

The problem is, what shall I buy?
Air Zookas or Scuba Scooters?
Rivers flowing around my mind,
Too much to choose from.
Hands everywhere with things to buy
Like an auction. Tenner, twenty, forty
Xbox 360, Subbuteo, PS3, even pooper scoopers
All in their hands.
We need a skip to carry them
Frantic hands to get the grasp of money.
What can I do?

And the houses standing there
In the pouring rain
Three bedroom, detached
With a security light
As the money falls out my pocket
To pay for it.

Kiaran Marsh (11)
Bishop Milner Catholic School, Dudley

Anthony's Blessing
(A poem written in the style of Imtiaz Dharker's 'Blessing' using characters from the text 'Millions' by Frank Cottrell-Boyce)

My eyes pop like a balloon
There's enough for everyone.

Imagine a quad bike
The roar of the engine
At the mud track
The voice of a clean engine.

The rush of money everywhere
Makes my adrenaline pump
The green cash in the bag
Makes angels sing
From bikes to PS3s to PlayStations too
Scuba Scooter, I'll buy the lot.
Tonnes of money in that bag.
I have to spend, spend, spend.
Thank you Damien for telling me this
I will never diss you again
Frantic legs, they were coming to tell me.

And the kids in the playground
Crowding around us
'Buy this!' 'Buy that!' they say
But I'm not listening
I have better things to buy
Because I have millions!

Nerissa Chater (12)
Bishop Milner Catholic School, Dudley

Anthony's Blessing
(A poem written in the style of Imtiaz Dharker's 'Blessing' using characters from the text 'Millions' by Frank Cottrell-Boyce)

The money should be mine
It's my destiny, who cares about giving to charity?

I've got to spend the money
In just sixteen days, how can I do it?
I have to hop around like a kangaroo
I think I could spend it at school.

I'm going to buy, buy, buy
Whatever I want
Because I've got the money
I could buy the bridge from Scotland to Ireland
Property, puppy, PSP, just some of the things
I could purchase with my money.
And with my diamond money
A quad bike could be mine
My money makes cash Jenga
As high as it could go
Before it comes tumbling down.

I'm going to buy a swimming pool
And a huge house
I don't care what Damian says
If he wants to give it to charity
He's better off dead.
So down to the shops I go.

Daniel Platt (12)
Bishop Milner Catholic School, Dudley

Anthony's Blessing
(A poem written in the style of Imtiaz Dharker's 'Blessing' using characters from the text 'Millions' by Frank Cottrell-Boyce)

Money falls from the sky
Look at the amount, I will die.

'Give it to the poor,' my brother says
But we could get a rocket, fly to the moon in days.
Think of all the stuff we could buy
After that we'll be big and high.

We could buy a massive house
But don't tell anyone, be as quiet as a mouse.
I know that our mom just died
Damien, he cried and cried
We can make it better now
But all he asks is how, how, how?
Our mom was like our world
Bright, beautiful and brilliant she was
Forget that, look at this property now
Shall we buy it? Yes or no?
I really like it, shall we go?

I suppose we could help the poor
But when we give them some, they will only ask for more
I would much rather buy something, something fun
But is it to be or not to be?
That is the question.

Matthew Holland (11)
Bishop Milner Catholic School, Dudley

I Ain't No Queen
(Inspired by 'Half-Caste' by John Agard)

I ain't no queen
'N' I a no fan of tea
Tha think I eat biscuits and cakes
With scones and butter
But ya see me now I am
As drunk as I can ever be.

I ain't no queen
'N' I a no fan of tea
Ya does think me likes to grow corps
'N' tamatas and patatas
But ya watch me now I ain't
Got no gar-din.

I ain't no queen
'N' I a no fan of tea
I ain't no Irish
With me green leprechaun hat.
I ain't no Scottish
With me fancy kilt.
I ain't no Welsh
With me rugby ball.

I ain't no queen
'N' I a no fan of tea
I ain't no English
'N' I ain't born from there
But I knows what it's like.

It ain't no la di da
And don't expect me to be
It ain't filled with rich snob
It's filled with rain
It ain't no walk in the park
But ya get used to et

I ain't no queen
And I ain't no fan of tea
Being posh is not me speciality
But being me
Is all I can be.

Munashe Muchena (13)
Bishop Milner Catholic School, Dudley

My Poem . . .
(Based on 'Stereotype' by John Agard)

I'm a full-blooded Black Country gal
A Sunday roast with tatos and yorkies, yum, yum, yum.
A saucer if tea in my hand,
Sitting having scones with my best friend, the Queen!
I live right by Buckingham Palace, in a huge, huge mansion.
When I get home I eat fish and chips from the local chippy.
Most of the time I'm spending money in London's high street,
Clothes, shoes and bags. Shopping with Gok Wan.
My other best friend is Simon Cowell;
I travel round the world with him like all the time.

Lydia Humphreys (13)

Bishop Milner Catholic School, Dudley

Anthony's Blessing
(A poem written in the style of Imtiaz Dharker's 'Blessing' using characters from the text 'Millions' by Frank Cottrell-Boyce)

All I want is money
Money and even more money.

Imagine what I could buy,
With all that money.
Top Trumps, even new football boots.
I wouldn't share it, I would keep it all to myself.

When the money fell out of the sky, I thought
What could we do with it?
Play games,
There are millions of games,
Cash Jenga,
Who can make the biggest tower?
When the tower falls, think of all those hands grabbing the money,
When the money falls I think of all the things I could do with it.
Spend it on my friends, I could even buy another Bonny.

When I found this money, I thought of all the people who need this wonderful money.
Damien would have said, 'Give it to the poor,'
I won't give it to the poor,
I wouldn't even give it to the police.

Daniel James (12)
Bishop Milner Catholic School, Dudley

English Women
(Based on 'Stereotype' by John Agard)

English women in the streets,
Hats and horses,
Drinking tea,
Beef and wine sauces . . .
Is that what you would expect to see?

English women in the streets,
Eating scones,
Whipped cream and jam,
British weather to moan,
Do you like green eggs and ham?

English women in the streets,
Four countries all have joined,
School book in hand,
A meal, set and dined . . .
Well it's time we took a stand!

English women in the streets,
'You' me all right kid!'
Hard work then chips for tea,
'Give us a quid!'
Well that's just me!

Kym Fitzpatrick (13)
Bishop Milner Catholic School, Dudley

I Remember . . .

What a time,
Being so young,
All those super memories,
I still taste them on my tongue.

I still see them in my mind,
I still hear them in my ears,
I can't believe I remember back,
Now I've gained these years.

I recall that special feeling,
Of being on top of the world,
After managing to tie my shoes,
A useful skill to learn.

That ropey feeling in my hand,
The burn of holding too tight,
And then the final victory,
'I've tied my shoes. Alright!'

I summon up the memory
Of my first dance class,
From the 'port de bras' to the 'reverence',
I hoped it'd last and last.

That memory, full of joy,
Of swimming with the dolphins,
Their leathery-soft skin gliding through our hands,
Our faces full of grins.

I see the scorching sunshine
Reflecting off the sea,
Making patterns in the water,
My heart was full of glee.

What a time,
Being so young,
All those super memories,
I still taste them on my tongue.

Hannah Dutton (12)
Cardinal Griffin Catholic High School, Cannock

In Mrs Windmill's Class

As the bell rang for class
Our first lesson was measuring mass
We measured this and measured that
And lastly measured a mat
The next lesson was painting
And I was bored of waiting
Then we went out for some fresh air
And after break I finished my bear
Our next lesson was French
And we did it outside so I sat on a bench
After French was lunch
And on my crisps I went munch
When we ate
We went outside to meet a mate
We played on the playground
And we went round and round
Our last lesson was good
All we did was play with wood
Then Mom rang on my phone
To say we have to walk home.

Danielle Austin (13)
Cardinal Griffin Catholic High School, Cannock

Kipper

The day I got my pet dog, Kipper,
Was when I was as young as five.
A little kitten-sized puppy,
Though this dog wasn't really alive.

He always smelt of pink roses,
Even when he rolled in the mud.
I would get Mum's special shampoo,
And wash him as much as I could.

I used to walk him to school,
And tie him to my chair.
If he didn't get attention,
Well that would be very rare.

When it was time to go home,
Everyone would pat my dog.
And if people forgot to say goodbye,
He would sit there sulking on a log.

By the time I got home from school,
And sat down in front of the telly.
Kipper told me it was time for feeding,
By rubbing his big round belly.

The sound of little Kipper's bark,
Was a sound I frequently heard.
Though I trained him extremely well,
To shut up with just one word.

My dog had lovely silky, white fur,
Fur as white as snow.
And if he ever got dirty,
That would make him feel low.

Now there's one thing I haven't mentioned about Kipper,
A fact that you wouldn't know.
That my little dog, Kipper,
Would never ever grow.

He always stayed a puppy,
He was always there for me.
But when I was too old to play with him,
He disappeared from me totally.

Victoria Hampton (13)
Cardinal Griffin Catholic High School, Cannock

Golden Eagle

I perch upon
The high rocks
In the scorching heat.
I wait for my next meal
To pass by my feet.
I track them down
With my sharp eyes.
I wait
It is quiet
I hurtle down
In the dusty clouds.
It's gone
It flutters away
I take off.
I am tired
I find a place to sleep.
Caves I think.
I haven't eaten yet,
I travelled towards
The horizon.
I sleep where I please
People try to get me
With a tube.
I'm quick
It missed
I'm scared
Back to the journey I think.

Zac Stanley (13)
Cardinal Griffin Catholic High School, Cannock

I Remember Those Days Well

I remember those days well,
The days I used to bake cakes.
Those days were good,
The days I used to bake cakes.

I would climb very high, on a chair,
Looking for extra special ingredients.
Out of the cupboard came chocolates and sweets,
Always too much to use!
Bowls and spoons would come flying out
Of the cupboards, so high.
I was ready now, very ready,
To bake cakes to my delight.

I would dump all the ingredients in a bowl,
Whizzing them round and round.
I wonder if they ever got dizzy,
Being whizzed round in that bowl.

The mixture was now ready,
But all that spinning made me hungry!
So I licked almost half out the bowl,
And this made my tummy feel funny!

They were now in the oven cooking,
Placed in by an adult of course.
I would sit and watch them grow higher,
Making sure they were rather good.

Out of the oven came golden cakes,
They looked so very yummy.
So I ate and ate and ate,
Until they were all in my tummy!

After eating all the cakes, it was time for washing up,
I hated the washing up, so I left it all for Mum!

I remember those days well,
The days I used to bake cakes.
Those days were good,
The days I used to bake cakes.

Sophie Fletcher (13)
Cardinal Griffin Catholic High School, Cannock

They Were The Times

They were the times
When all I had to worry about was food and play.
I never had to think about what to write or say.
My teachers in primary school would put funny stickers in my book,
My brother would always get me covered in muck.
When I thought of it, 13 seemed like miles away,
It's weird that all of this seems like yesterday.
So many memories, most happy, a few sad.
Always being squeezed and nicknamed 'Braveheart' by Dad.
From dance and stagecoach to my friend dying so sadly,
How I dealt with some things well and others very badly.
From wearing Teletubbie leggings to Levi jeans and New Look tops.
From wanting to play in the park all day to just wanting to shop.
The Teletubbie toast and Santa, the tooth fairy too,
Sticking down feathers, being covered in glue.
An astronaut at six, a chef at eight,
Putting plastic food on a plastic plate.
Thinking that boys had a disease and burping was a crime,
In cops and robbers I always did my time.
My first day at school with my Barbie bag and pencil case,
I never ever wanted to play kiss chase.
I remember wanting teddy bears and dolls galore,
Then getting shouted at for them being on the floor.
Me and my friends were always going to be in a band,
Singing our songs on the playground hand in hand.
I have grown up since then, I am now a teen.
I no longer colour for fun or to my brother am I mean.
I still enjoy playing make-believe now and again,
Being a pilot and flying my own plane.
Now I have school to worry about with tests and more,
And I will have to tidy it up if something falls on the floor,
Although I am growing up and make a bit more mess,
I sometimes like to still pretend I am a princess.
On the outside I am 13 and you can see,
But on the inside I am still a child and always will be.
Yes . . .
They were the times.

Hannah Hale (13)
Cardinal Griffin Catholic High School, Cannock

My Best Friend

I made sure he had a seat,
A seat all of his own,
Where he could sit and stare,
And watch the wild unknown.

His eyes glared black as coal,
But his stubbly brown hair softened him up,
His plump, round belly was like jumping in mud,
His white nose was like a little rosebud,
He smelt like melted chocolate,
And he felt like stroking a big, fat cat,
When he moved he made not a sound,
I especially liked that,
His ears could hear everything,
Every secret I ever told,
Every song I ever sang,
Every worry I ever had,
He knew how to solve everything,
Without saying a single word,
His hands were always firmly locked in mine,
Wherever we went,
I knew on the palm of my hand he would be stood,
His little feet dragged on the floor,
Getting dirtier with each step,
He stood small as an ant, but was always big to me,
Then we stopped, Mum shouted,
'Come on!'
I ran to catch her up,
As I got off and the bus ran away,
My heart sank.

I still remember that day,
Still very clearly now,
That was the day I lost my best friend
My best friend, that was my teddy bear.

Ariana Foley (13)
Cardinal Griffin Catholic High School, Cannock

Memories From The Past

In my mind they wait,
Memories from the past,
Wait for me to think,
Then they come so fast.

Seven years old, my first party,
The sweet smell of a birthday cake I did thrive.
My friends arrive,
Lying in wait to see that float
Then all aboard that floating boat,
We swam and played and had some fun
Then, to touch the side when we were done.

Tiggy, the stray tabby cat, came when I was nine,
She didn't cost a penny at the time
She feels so soft
As soft as a feather.
There she is bouncing in and out of heather.

Eleven years old, my presentation arrived
The feel of awkwardness was in the room.
But I was still on the dance floor doing a 'jive'
I won, won the floor, I also won a trophy with the horse I adore.

I was twelve when Bobby died,
The taste of bitter tears was in the air
The whole house felt bare
Everyone was so kind.

These are some of my memories
Some, I shared with friends.
I continue to grow them.
My journey never ends.

Nikita Del-Giudice (13)
Cardinal Griffin Catholic High School, Cannock

The Listeners

It was a cold night.
There was a full moon out and the sky was jet-black.
The tall trees stood swaying side to side and the wind was whistling.
There was a small, ruined cottage sitting by the polluted river.

Suddenly the noise of a horse galloping could be heard in the distance.
The noise got louder but this time it was a man shouting, 'Yah, yah.'
The man was whipping the horse on the hip,
Trying to make it go faster than it could.

'Whoa!' the man shouted and the horse began to slow down.
When they got closer to the cottage,
Horse stopped as fast as he could and refused to go anywhere near the house.
It was like he could sense something was wrong inside there.

So the man jumped off the horse and took out a piece of rope, and tied him to the nearest tree.
He slowly walked over to the cottage and found the door was open slightly.
He heard a loud noise but as he turned around, he found it was just the horse sitting down.

He carried on and walked in through the old wooden door.
Inside was just an empty room with a candle and box in the corner.
He walked up the old stairs.
Then *bang!*

The man went inside the cottage to try and see what was upsetting the horse,
But he never returned.

Faye Louise Harvey (13)
Cardinal Griffin Catholic High School, Cannock

Childhood Fantasy

I've turned thirteen
And hate the responsibilities that come with it
My freedom has increased
But fun and games have decreased
Pressurised by magazines
I love riding in limousines!
Make-up and doing up my hair
Now I find it cool to be fair.

My imaginary mice
That never got lice
With itchy chickenpox
And cute, shiny locks
Dressing up Barbies
And pretend tea parties
If I had one wish
I would of asked for a fish.

Kiss chase, tig and stuck in the mud
Then falling over with a humungous thud
Going to my magic place
Dressed in the finest satin lace
Pretending to be cooks
Making cities out of books
I remember my sister being such a bore
But neither of us are a child anymore.

Shannon Collins (13)
Cardinal Griffin Catholic High School, Cannock

The Volcano

When the deadly volcano erupts
The boiling ash spreads.
When the powerful rumble goes in the sky
People stop and stare at the ash in the air.
Massive clumps of white dust people see
As some of the volcano crashes down into the sea.

Abby Marie Liddington (13)
Cardinal Griffin Catholic High School, Cannock

The Listeners!

Knock, knock, knock
As the traveller knocked at the door,
The noise echoed through the woods
As he bellowed words of pain.

Yet young Prince Todd got no reply,
And silence surged softly backwards,
And when he knocked on the door again a second time,
He felt as if his heart had frozen.

The house lay darkly upon the hard terrain,
And dusk was filling the sky,
And young Prince Todd heard a crash,
As he peeked through the opening door.

His horse was gone before the prince could catch,
His split stirrup leather lay neatly on the ground,
And young Prince Todd was left alone,
And he was never found!

Villagers hear him cry at night,
They hear him crying with pain,
And next time you go in woods at night,
Try not to be afraid!

Polly Smith (12)
Cardinal Griffin Catholic High School, Cannock

My Primary School

My primary school was great
I wasn't sure about the assemblies
But I made loads of mates
I always played football and other sports
I played in many courts
I tried to get in the top set
But I was always at the bottom
With the rest!
But overall I enjoyed primary school!

Ben Chamberlin (13)
Cardinal Griffin Catholic High School, Cannock

My Poem

I've got the football to play,
I'm at school all day,
I've got the English to learn,
All the pages to turn.

I feel the music beat,
Let me move my feet,
We run around and around,
Until the sun goes down.

I've got to tidy my room,
I sweep with the broom,
My mom is sound,
She drives me round and round.

My bike is broken,
The window is open,
My car blows smoke,
I think it is broke.

I'm going to have shower,
My ice skates are Bauer,
My bike is GT
I like watching TV.

Connor Butcher (13)
Cardinal Griffin Catholic High School, Cannock

Lion

I wake up in the middle of a desert.
Having no home day after day.
When I wake up I'm somewhere different all the time
And I can't find food every night.
In the desert is where I belong.

I'm always feeling very hot.
There is very little shade to go in.
So most of the time I stay in the grass.
I always feel very sleepy.

I'm a very ear-splitting creature.

You can barely hear any bird, that is how quiet it is.
People try to attack me.
Sometimes I scare them away but they can't get any closer with my loud roar.
I'm always very lonely.
I am a very fast animal, I always jump across from one part of the grass to another.
I am the only lion in the desert.

Michael Rose (13)
Cardinal Griffin Catholic High School, Cannock

Giraffe

As the wind blows among the trees,
I camouflage myself in the dark green bush,
I wait for the fierce beasts to spring out at me.

I reach out with my long neck to grab some leaves,
I munch, I chew, I hear a crackling along the dry dead twigs
On the deserted path.

I see paw prints as big as my enemies,
I run for my life - he's chasing after me.

The boiling sun sizzling on my skin,
I eat more leaves from the tallest tree.

Imogen Jones (11)
Cardinal Griffin Catholic High School, Cannock

Soph's Poem

The sunny days,
At our school,
Nice to each other,
That was our rule!

The good days,
That we have,
What great memories,
They were never bad!

Children playing,
All around,
As the sun was shining,
On the green, luscious ground!

Delicious food,
Up in the air,
The children ran,
From everywhere!

Sophie Palmer (13)
Cardinal Griffin Catholic High School, Cannock

Primary School

P laying with friends
R E was great
I n the playground with my mates
M y best friends were the best
A nd I liked rest
R estless days
Y awn all the way

S cience was a piece of cake
C areful not to be late
H olidays never ended
O ur things were always mended
O ur teacher told us to shhhhhhh
L istening as much as we could.

Natasha Woodall (12)
Cardinal Griffin Catholic High School, Cannock

My Poem!

I've got to get out of bed
And not rest my head
Wash my face
Then I'm outta this place.

Catch the bus
While in a rush
Take a seat
And put up my feet.

Arrive at school
And not the pool
Looking very cool!

Meet my friends
Then grab my pens
Get to class
First lesson is . . . maths! *Zzz!*

Shannon Malone (13)
Cardinal Griffin Catholic High School, Cannock

My Primary School Poem

In Miss Moore's class
There was no war whatsoever
Because we all acted quite so clever!
We all had smiles spring from our faces
As we began the sports day races
The shiny charts
With the sticky stars
Pupils ran as fast as cars
As we waited in line to pay
Our dinner money
Pupils went mad
To see what we had!
And when circle time came
It was never a pain.

Morgan Challinor (12)
Cardinal Griffin Catholic High School, Cannock

Eruptions

Very explosive and dangerous
On the inside it has so much
Action with the hot lava flowing
Loud and destructive
Constructive, quiet and unknown
Awaiting the eruption is
Frightening and scary,
Evacuations and alerts.
Never do the volcanoes go away,
They will erupt forever.
On the inside a destructive
Eruption building strength
Every second.
On the outside an explosion of
Lava and a devastation to
Its surroundings.

Sam Hollingmode (13)
Cardinal Griffin Catholic High School, Cannock

Untitled

I've got my clothes to prepare
Now wash my hair
Ready for school
Got to follow the rule
The weather is a bit nippy
I am going to the chippy
I want a fritter
But it is a bit bitter
Now I need a Coke
Cos I am a bloke
I always have a shiver
Because I have no liver
I've got to go to the bath
I walked barefoot on the path.

Luke Round (11)
Cardinal Griffin Catholic High School, Cannock

The Volcano

While it sleeps through the night,
Desperate to burst with rage,
The volcano grumbles,
While the crowd starts to stare,
The sun rises and the volcano gives up . . .

It bursts with fire splattering everywhere,
People roaring, scared to the bone,
Shivering children, hiding in cramped corners,
Not knowing what is going to happen,
The dull sky is dark, looking like there's a hidden monster . . .

The huge volcano is never-ending,
Still covering the Earth with its poison,
Days yet to end, bubbling and fiery,
Nearby animals rushing home,
As the volcano is still lashing out . . .

Sofie Jones (13)
Cardinal Griffin Catholic High School, Cannock

Adults' Work

I've got my breakfast to eat
And clean the seat
Gotta clean my teeth
And see to Keith
The fridge to mend
Some letters to send
Gotta go for a walk
And defrost the pork
Gotta feed dogs
Fetch some logs
Need to go to the shops
And see the cops.
Now it's time to sleep,
My memories I'll keep.

Emily Fellows (11)
Cardinal Griffin Catholic High School, Cannock

Steven's Work

I've got my breakfast to eat,
I'll have some meat,
I have a wash,
I get dressed really posh,
I have some money for school,
My brothers look really cool,
We go to Cardinal Griffin,
On the way there I start sniffing,
When we go home,
We all have a moan,
I have my tea,
We all get a pea,
We go to bed,
I say goodnight to my ted, Fred.

Steven Edwards (12)
Cardinal Griffin Catholic High School, Cannock

Courtney's Work!

A sister to look after
She always eats pasta
I went to school
After going to the pool
Going to Cannock
But my mates cause a havoc
Go home
I'm all alone
Dinner to prepare
I want to go to the fair
Go to bed
After I bumped my head
My uncle comes round, he is Mick
And my mom has been sick.

Courtney Targett (12)
Cardinal Griffin Catholic High School, Cannock

Chantelle's Day

I've got the English to learn
The pages to turn
The writing in the class
Then go to Mass
Then lunch to eat
The music for the beat
Clean my room
Sweep with the broom
Then the homework to do
That's boring too
Another day gone by
Mustn't lose my tie
It's time to sleep
And then I had cold feet.

Chantelle Gunner (13)
Cardinal Griffin Catholic High School, Cannock

Primary School

P laying on the field
R unning around like mad
I maginative writing
M ad people running all over the playground
A ggressive boys
R olling down the hill
Y elling when you get tigged.

S houting for no reason at the top of your voice
C hasing people, trying to tig them
H ide-and-seek
O nly people in Year 6 and 5 allowed on the top field
O nly letting cool people play bulldog
L aying on the grass relaxing.

Danielle White (11)
Cardinal Griffin Catholic High School, Cannock

Primary School

P laying with your friends
R unning wild in the playground
I n our school we all play nicely
M y friends are all very nice
A noraks are what we wear when it rains
R unning boys playing kiss chase
Y oung children learning subjects

S nowball fights in the winter
C homping on chocolate at break time
H aving not a lot of homework
O ld teachers teaching us skills
O ranges are given at break time
L ovely school meals by the cook.

Tamara Hillman (11)
Cardinal Griffin Catholic High School, Cannock

Primary School

Maths
The teacher teaches you stupid chants,
And I just think, *this lesson is pants!*

English
The lesson is so very boring,
Leading to very loud snoring!

PE
Today the teacher made us play cricket,
I did a perfect bowl and hit the wicket!

RE
Religious Education, what a doss,
Our teacher thinks she's the boss!

Paul Brewster (11) & Owen Wilkes (12)
Cardinal Griffin Catholic High School, Cannock

Me Going Out

I sweep up hair in a shop
Sometimes I think I'm gonna drop
My feet are sore
I am so bored
When I get home I brush my hair with a comb
I have a shower then go to the snow dome
I meet Abbie there with her hair everywhere
I eat some cheese
I say, 'More please!'
Take a chill pill
Because you are ill, ill
I'm saying goodbye
Because you are a fly.

liona Kilgallon (12)
Cardinal Griffin Catholic High School, Cannock

The Volcano

O volcano, o volcano
Please don't explode on me
O volcano, o volcano
Please leave us be.

O volcano, o volcano
I'm scared of your volcanic ash
O volcano, o volcano
We do not want our homes to have a bash.

O volcano, o volcano
Make sure you don't explode now
O volcano, o volcano
As we say goodbye for now.

James Roberts (12)
Cardinal Griffin Catholic High School, Cannock

An Elephant's Food

An elephant is comin' to the tree,
Stomp, stomp, stomp.
It's comin' to eat the leaves,
Stomp, stomp, stomp.
It's comin' to eat the branches,
It's comin' to eat you!

It's comin' to its baby,
Stomp, stomp, stomp.
Bringin' its food to its baby,
Stomp, stomp, stomp.
It's bringin' you to its baby,
Run, run, run away.

Kate Hawkins (12)
Cardinal Griffin Catholic High School, Cannock

Volcano

The fiery beast
Is like death and doom
You run and hide
But it always finds
Nowhere to go
Apart from Hell
So you might as well
Plead, plead, plead
The heavens won't help
So go to sleep
Your death is
Upon you.

Ryan Di Cesare (12)
Cardinal Griffin Catholic High School, Cannock

Primary Poem

You walk into school and you look very cool.
You go into class and you turn very sad,
Then you see your friends and everything's alright.

At break you have your milk and fruit,
You run around and you play with mud.
At the end of the day
You walk out of school still looking very cool.
You had a good day,
It was really fun,
Now it's time for you to go home.

Don't miss your school!

Monika Bednarczyk & Lara Morris (13)
Cardinal Griffin Catholic High School, Cannock

Volcano

The volcano exploded,
The sun imploded,
You are dead,
While in bed,
The lava pouring out,
It's all about,
When I ran away,
There was a huge play,
About today,
This dreaded Wednesday.

Edward Page (13)
Cardinal Griffin Catholic High School, Cannock

Your Whisper

I can hear your whisper in the wind,
Your whisper in my ear.

Your silent echo in the air,
I long to hear your prayer.

Your wish upon a shooting star,
Your lullaby, your song, not far.

I can't believe you cannot see
Your whisper belongs to me.

Megan Walker (12)
Cardinal Griffin Catholic High School, Cannock

Gone

The silence, how it kills me
Although I'm still alive.
The misty, bitter, cold air
Although I'm still warm-blooded.

The deadness that surrounds me
Although alive, I'm on my own.
The positive thoughts in my head
Although it's the negative ones I show.

The colours are slowly fading
Although they're still so bright.
The darkness arrives
Although the night has already fallen.

The dead are awake
Although they are asleep.
The actions they do
Although they lie there still.

Even though I can see them
They are gone. Forever gone.

Bethany Wood (13)
Churnet View Middle School, Leek

How Times Move On!
(In remembrance of Patricia, Samantha And Marcus Carter)

Four years gone by since you passed away
So beautiful and young
But taken away so tragic
A million tears, another million to come,
I sit and wonder, *where has time gone?*

I loved your smiles, I loved your laughs
I miss you, I miss your smile.
And to be honest,
I still shed a tear every once in a while.

I know where you need to be,
Even though you're not here with me,
Everything you do, everything you did
Every trace of you got taken away
Within a second, and I still pray
That you could stay forever and a day.

How time ticks, how years go by,
It hurts every moment,
You not being at my side,
I wish you were, I really do and
Always remember, I love you!

Now you're in Heaven, all my tears flow
In my heart you will never go,
Neither will the times we shared and the
Times we were scared,
We were there for each other then
And always will be!

There have been moments when I needed you here,
But I know you can't be.
As much as you would like to sit here with me,
The memories I will never let go
I need you to know.

You had many titles -
My best friend, my cousin
We will reunite in years to come
But for now my darling,

Rest peaceful, I love you!

In remembrance of
Patricia Carter   9-11-1995 - 6-3-2006
Samantha Carter   13-5-1989 - 6-3-2006
Marcus Carter   31-7-1998 - 6-3-2006

Ella Cope (13)
Churnet View Middle School, Leek

Just Behind That Door

I am the tide that ebbs and flows,
Across the midst of time.
Think of me, I'm all around,
I am the bells that chime.

I am the breeze that softly blows,
Across the barren moor.
Think of me, I'm all around,
I am just behind that door.

I am the thought that's in your head,
Whilst pondering the day.
Think of me, I'm all around,
To help you on your way.

I am the star that's in the sky,
Throughout the scarlet night.
Think of me, I'm all around,
I know it's hard, don't cry.

I am the voice that echoes,
Throughout the silent room.
Think of me I'm all around,
I am the flowers that bloom.

As you fall asleep at night,
I softly stroke your brow.
Think of me, I'm all around,
Sleep well, my love, rest now.

Robert Alexander (12)
Churnet View Middle School, Leek

Dark Days

Even though I think,
My life is worthless,
Some things also should be savoured,
No one thinks twice about me,
But I soldier on in belief,
That one day I will rise again,
Bloodshot eyes and fathomless spirit.
Exploring havoc,
Destruction lies on every path,
But that will not matter,
For every death,
There is a life,
This pain must end now,
All suffering to be obliterated,
Because if it does not,
My heart,
My soul,
My passion,
Will mean nothing,
Walking on broken glass,
Leaving nothing,
But a shattered past,
Shooting blindly,
As I lumber on,
With vengeful rage,
Vanquishing innocence,
Because these dark days,
Will last for all eternity.

Robert Salt (13)
Churnet View Middle School, Leek

Friends

We've been together for years now,
Been broken up by boys,
Best friends forever,
Even amongst all the noise.

People say things that hurt your feelings,
But we don't mind,
But it's when we start healing,
We are hard to find.

Nothing is ever serious,
When we are together,
It's all one big laugh,
Together forever.

When we fall out,
It's never for long,
We always say sorry,
That's 'cause we belong.

It takes more than caring,
To be a real friend
The nature of friendship;
Requires a blend.

You are my friend,
Through thick and thin,
I'm glad you're my best friend,
You bring out the *me* within.

Natalie Stacie Wilson (12)
Churnet View Middle School, Leek

The Night-Time

A silvery velvet stream in the sky,
Lasts up to twelve hours - yet doesn't quite die,
Little twinkles and shines light the gloomy dark,
The black turns to grey in the still, silent park,
Although it's quite frightening, although I am afraid,
I move not one inch - no left nor right turn is made.

Travel on through the slightly-lit streets,
No two people are out; so no two people meets,
Vast shadows are cast by each tall, immense house,
Yet inside, nothing moves, nothing speaks - not a mouse,
I move along steadily, at a snail's pace,
Making my way back home, back to my base.

Perhaps in the morning, I will tell my mum
Because she would never say I was being dumb,
Then again, she may not believe my story,
Of magic, mystique and a light-show of glory,
I'll keep it a secret; yes, that's what I'll do,
And maybe one day someone else can experience the night too.

Mischa Balderstone (13)
Churnet View Middle School, Leek

The Dreaded C Word

Cancer, the word rings through my ears,
Cancer, it was all my greatest fears,
Cancer, it seemed ever so frightening,
Then it hit us like lightning.

Cancer, now it's here with my mum, it may not go away . . .
Cancer, it's stayed for a while . . . we've nearly chased it away,
Cancer, it ruined our lives for a while.
Now we've polished it off with a great big smile.

Cancer, it's been such a very long journey,
Cancer, with all the confusing therapy,
Cancer, I can't wait until the end,
Not long now my friend!

We all cannot wait until
The end!

I love you Mum!

Rebecca Bennett (13)
Churnet View Middle School, Leek

Rethink, Reuse, Recycle - Really?

Left lying listlessly
Litter duvets the corners of our lives
Pinned, pointlessly peering
Under the guillotine gates
Wrappers relentlessly raging
Like a tsunami of waste
Diseased, deadly
Doomed creatures
Suffocated, strangled
By the sea of 'a litter nation'.

Do we really want our
World to turn into a
Mirror of greed?

Molly Belfield (13)
Churnet View Middle School, Leek

Happiness

Happiness is like soft vanilla ice cream,
It tastes like BBQ spare ribs,
It smells like sizzling sausages,
It looks like a hot day in Jamaica,
It sounds like relaxation music,
It feels like a lovely warm hug,
It is the colour of sky-light blue.

Alex Plumb (13)
Hallmoor Special School, Birmingham

Three Witches Talking To Macbeth

Three witches, mysterious, smelly and spotty, talking to Macbeth.
Three witches, skinny, wrinkled and sneering, talking to Macbeth.
Three witches, warty, disgusting and weird, talking to Macbeth.
Three witches, evil, devilish and scary, talking to Macbeth.
Three witches, stinking, ugly and diseased, talking to Macbeth.

Sean O'Brien (13)
Hallmoor Special School, Birmingham

Happiness

Happiness is waking up and going ice skating,
Happiness is going out with my friends and playing on my Xbox 360,
Happiness is playing football in the garden and riding my bike,
Happiness is kissing your girlfriend and BBQs with your family.

Luke Roney (13)
Hallmoor Special School, Birmingham

Weather - Haiku

It was cold today,
It was breezy yesterday,
Tomorrow - sunshine.

Jordan Emerson (13)
Hallmoor Special School, Birmingham

Football - Haiku

Football is the best,
Running around, kicking ball,
Goalie saving balls.

Katherine Colbert (13)
Hallmoor Special School, Birmingham

Spider - Haiku

Spider spinning web,
Spiders catch flies in silk web,
Munching fifty flies.

Shaun Betts (13)
Hallmoor Special School, Birmingham

Me - Haiku

Wrestling is so cool
Bell Heath, a really great trip
Katie Price - pretty!

Haroon Ansar (13)
Hallmoor Special School, Birmingham

The Captain

The captain has scars on his face
A belt on his waist
His heart as cold as the winter snow
And once you meet him it will show!

He fights like a knight
His breath smells of fright
He fights to the bitter end
Just to defend
His loyal ship.

Daniel Managhan (11)
Haute Vallee School, Jersey

The Chamber

I was one of the stronger ones,
That was taken into camp.
The Jewish blood warm in my veins,
Feeling anxious, my forehead damp.

They told us, 'Work will keep you alive,'
As we all feared for our life.
But it was all a lie, I realised,
When I was taken from my wife.

My children forced to work 'til death,
Everyone fought to stay alive.
But what was the point? We were worthless,
Anyway we were all to die.

The shooting, the gassing, the burning,
Starvation, skin and bones.
What did I do to have a life like this?
All I wanted was to be home.

I hated it there; I didn't know myself anymore,
I was a stranger.
It was the last day of my life,
The day I was taken into the chamber.

Chantalle Roberts (14)
Haute Vallee School, Jersey

My Hero

My hero is Dad.
Dad is better than ever.
When I need someone,
Dad's always there for me.
I have always loved Dad and Dad has always loved me.
My hero is my dad, it will always and always be Dad.
He's never far, he's close
He will always be in my heart
My hero is Dad.

Lisa Jaremyn (12)
Haute Vallee School, Jersey

Marley, Lennon And Dylan

Three magic men,
Who've changed the face of music,
Two of them dead,
But their legacy lives on,
Three iconic men,
From three iconic countries,
Marley from Jamaica,
With his Rasta man dreads,
Lennon from England,
With his little round specs,
Dylan from America,
With his harmonica,
These are the men,
Rated ten out of ten,
Bob Marley, John Lennon, Bob Dylan.

Joe Birrell (14)
Haute Vallee School, Jersey

The World Cup

Fighting it out like a war,
Instead of guns using a football,
Countries from the four corners of the world,
All this for a cup made from gold,
It's not just a game,
It's a battle of strength, wits and beliefs,
In a second, a whole country's hopes can be shattered,
You're a hero, if you score,
But if you miss, I won't say anymore
As I said, all this for a cup of gold,
It's more than that,
It's knowing you're the best team in the whole wide world!

Daniel Robinson (14)
Haute Vallee School, Jersey

Losing Someone Close

Memories in my head
Of all the good things said
From good to bad
From grief to relief
But I know my gran's not coming back.
She was so close to me
Half my heart is empty
What will I do?
I'm lost without you
Please come back to me
I've just lost someone so close.

Nikita Binet (13)
Haute Vallee School, Jersey

Football

F ootie is fun
O n a pitch or a playground
O n a beach or in a car park
T -shirts all sweaty
B all in the middle, ready to start
A ll players are nervous, trembling heart
L ong ball to the goalkeeper
L ands on top of the goal.

Dominik Jagla (12)
Haute Vallee School, Jersey

Dreams

My dreams are in the Titanic,
My happiness lives in the sea,
My anger curls up in the rock,
While my love is left to run free.

Alex Langlois (13)
Haute Vallee School, Jersey

Football

F ootball is the best
O ther sports are cool as well but
O ften I watch football
T he World Cup is about to start
B razil will probably win
A frica might lose but
L ots of people are going to watch
L ots of players kicking a ball!

José Roberto Pestana (12)
Haute Vallee School, Jersey

The World Cup

The world will be full with cheer
Leather balls will be lifted in the air
Everyone will sing a song while the players come out
What a wonderful event it is going to be
Over 95 million people watch the World Cup
The stairs are going to rattle
And the ball goes off and everyone races for the ball.

Kevin Aubignac (12)
Haute Vallee School, Jersey

Love

L ove is a wonderful thing
O nly if you don't break someone's heart
V enezuela is the place for love
E ven if you don't get along.

Alfie Ashpole (11)
Haute Vallee School, Jersey

Young Love - Thanks To Cupid Above
(I write this poem/rap song about the girl that I care for, Rebekah Sarah Jones)

Rebekah, I'm glad I met ya, I regret if I ever upset ya,
Things may have been better if I didn't give you my letter,
If only I knew you better,
I remember when I first met her, she was wearing a green sweater,
She was a redhead, her beauty muted me,
She's so cute I wish you could see.
I wanted her to be with me, we'd be free,
We'd walk across the sand and I'd hold her hand and watch the sea.
It sounds so grand,
Understand that you're worth more to me than the world's economy,
You belong with me, you were a bomb to me,
As beautiful as a girl could be,
I could be your bee and you my honey,
That I'd collect and protect in my tree,
That sounds a bit funny.

Josh Hamilton (15)
Heronsbridge Special School, Bridgend

Bastogne

For countless damnèd days we held that pass,
Upon which German shells rained down en masse.

Steel on flesh, for all could hear the roar,
As another soldier, motionless, hit the floor.

Day and night we struggled through the cold,
And for their efforts some will ne'er grow old.

The pure white winter snow incarnadine,
Shed from those who for our freedom died.

So pray a while for those who won't come home,
For those who won't return from bloodied Bastogne.

Nick Edmonds (15)
King Edward VI School, Stratford-upon-Avon

Holiday

Crusty ruined boats moving in the docks,
The rough sea is like banging on old raggedy rocks.
As you walk along the golden sand
Watching people arrive for the evening band.
People reaching over the ice cream van
'What would you like my dear?' asks the man.
Everyone says, 'I don't mind,'
Just to make the man think they're kind.
Slotting in their money
Trying to win a prize,
Really they're not being very wise.

Walking in shops to get a bucket and spade,
'Can I have my money?'
'I've already paid,
For goodness sake, I have, I have.'
Oh what a to-do, oh what a to-do
I may as well go and sit on the loo,
No one believes me they don't, they don't,
I will not let them get away with this, I won't, I won't!

Back in the shop
With my cop
I won, I won,
It was a con.

Time to go home
It's been a long day
I hope that I know the way
I can't wait to get home
And go to bed
Ready for another day
At the seaside.
Maybe this time I will just watch the tide.

Ellie Hickson (12)
North Leamington School, Leamington Spa

Dad

You left me without my rock
You broke my heart in two
When I saw you lying there
I didn't know what to do
That day just feels like yesterday
When I saw you lying there
Lying pale, weak and slim
And not a strand of hair
The times we had were mind-blowing
I remember them to the day
Going to the footie,
And our team winning the game.

I remember the day you held me
Held me in your arms
And then the day I held your hands
And your sweaty palms
I remember when you used to stroke my brow
And I did the same
When you announced you had cancer
My life began to change.
24 hours a day I was worried about you sick
I didn't want you to leave me
Yet if I had a choice to pick
I remember saying to you,
'Are you going to die?'
And your response always was,
'No I will survive.'

I remember the day you passed away
And the very last words you said were,
'Amy I love you, I always have,
You're my little princess.'

Amy Biggs (11)
North Leamington School, Leamington Spa

Private Allen

He was horrified; having second thoughts.
His head was buzzing.
He heard a voice, 'Jump, jump.'
Suddenly, tumbling to the ground
Fumbling for the button,
The button, the button
Aha, he found the button
Now just the waiting;
The wind in his ears;
The pounding of his heart.
Now his eyes shut and all was quiet.

A man from the army; Sergeant Zieger
'Man down, he's in the water!'
A blinding flash.

Private Allen opened his eyes
He was alone.
Alone on a beach.
Alone on a beach on an island.
He heard a buzz, buzz, buzz.
He heard a bang; loud footsteps,
He opened his eyes.
Aliens!
Aliens staring at him.
Aliens staring at him, alone on a beach on an island.
'Get up,' said the alien.
'No,' said Private Allen.
He grabbed his gun; two bullets in the barrel.
Cracked the trigger twice
And then his head exploded.

Sebastian Stuart (12)
North Leamington School, Leamington Spa

A Helping Hand

The room is hot and stuffy.
I sit there in the heat
My head is sore
My mouth is dry
I stare down at my sheet.

The questions are impossible
They swirl around in my head
Why am I in school today?
I wish I'd stayed in bed!

These words, they mean nothing
I just don't understand
I wish I was brave enough
To ask for a helping hand.

The others are so clever
Scribbling words down
Their shoulders hunched
Their minds set
And me, I'm just a clown.

The teacher wanders over
My palms start to sweat
What do I do now? I think
The hardest question yet.

She leans over my shoulder
She tuts at my lack of work
'Outside now!' she shouts
The others just sit and smirk.

Rachel Wells (11)
North Leamington School, Leamington Spa

Who Said Grown Men Don't Cry?

There I stood, clashing swords
Fighting to defeat the five lords
Helping me,
A top archer and a top friend,
Moriki,
As the wolves attack,
I knew
I had to act,
Dodging every claw and sword.
I saw
I could see no more.
We put our weapons away,
Then ran rapidly, racing in rage
Over the barren wasteland.

Suddenly, out of the flat death field,
One of the five lords appeared.
I drew my sword, the ground shook
I fell, another emerged Moriki shot two
It dropped to the floor.
I looked at my leg
It was marrow, bone marrow
In a flash Moriki dropped his arrow
A blade cut through him like butter,
And he fell on the toast
I pulled my sword out and stabbed the oh mighty one.

As he entered the heavens,
A wet tear dripped down my face.

Charlie Jackson (11)
North Leamington School, Leamington Spa

Tobey Jacks

My mum has just told me,
About her new sweet shop,
It's right round the corner,
From a local car park,
I'm really excited,
I want it to open,
I guess I will have to
Wait for a bit.

It has been three months now
Since I shouted wow!
Because the new sweet shop
Has really blown my head off,
Just two months to go,
Until everyone starts to flow,
Right into Tobey Jacks,
To get lots of sweets and cakes.

Finally it's open!
My heart is beating faster,
Everyone is coming,
To get some lovely sweets,
I really can't wait,
Until it's really famous,
I'm feeling really happy,
I think I might faint.

George Want (12)
North Leamington School, Leamington Spa

Zero To Hero

Oh Bendtner, oh Bendtner, you never let us down,
In the important games, us Arsenal fans never frown,

Your sheer brilliance in front of goal,
But to be honest, you're never on a roll,

One game you're good, the next you're not,
One game you score none, the next a lot,

On your good days, you're like Drogba, you hardly miss,
Your goals - like his are just pure bliss,

But on your bad days, how do you miss? You only know that,
And the crowd all shout, 'My gran could have scored that!'

When you're subbed, I'm never upset,
Because one too many times you've missed the net

Sometimes I wish you could be good - but I'm afraid it seems,
That could only happen in my dreams!

You need a decent celebration fast,
Please, try and forget about your woeful past,

Try to look ahead to your glory days (if you ever have any)
To when you score goals, you may score many,

Hopefully one day, you will go from zero to . . .
Hero!

Kyle Joyce (11)
North Leamington School, Leamington Spa

There Are No Winners In War

War is a dreadful eyesore,
It is filled with lots of gore.
With men and women screaming in pain,
Because they were horrifically maimed,
As the sky let loose its bloody rain,
While soldiers are shooting at each other,
Mourning men carry their bleeding brothers,
War contains terrible, cruel violence,
Then there's a sudden silence . . .

Fighting on the battlefield,
The bloodstained ground covered with corpses,
Laying on the floor a proud banner with a golden shield,
We have all lost.

Both sides have suffered casualties,
Soldiers who fought have gained injuries,
Children cry for the loss of their fathers.
Some men go home petrified of the horrors they saw,
For evermore they will remember the gore,
For the blood on their hands will never wash.
War is a serious and mortifying experience.

Tom Harvey (12)
North Leamington School, Leamington Spa

Not Tired

Well now, are you happy?
I'm in bed with my teddy!
I've brushed my teeth, I'm counting sheep,
I am not being snappy!

You nag, nag,
Blame it . . . all . . . on . . . me
When . . . I . . . am . . . eight . . . ee . . . n
Zzzzzzzz . . .

Daniela Cowell (11)
North Leamington School, Leamington Spa

That Desert Island

That desert island
The bright blue sky
Caught the corner of my eye.

That desert island
The beaming sun
Was like a huge spotlight.

That desert island,
The warm, golden sand
Running through my toes.

That desert island
Calm and steady sea water
Glistening in the scalding sun.

That desert island
The green, tall palm trees
Swaying in the peaceful breeze.

That desert island,
All calm and peaceful,
Not one person in sight.

Jade Killingbeck (12)
North Leamington School, Leamington Spa

The Feelings Of Death

The world is a blur around me
If we win this the world is free.

Slice, jab, thrust, cut,
My mind's on autopilot.

A soft thump and I fall down screaming
A single arrow and my thigh is bleeding

My wife, my son, all slipping away,
Above me undisturbed goes on the fray.

And the white tunnel approaches.

Gregor Fletcher (11)
North Leamington School, Leamington Spa

Parents, Parents!

I'm ten years old,
And my parents nag me,
Why can't they let me be?
They say, 'Clean your room,
Sweep the floor with a broom.'
I wish I could escape to Italy,
To get some rest so that they won't nag me.

They listen to you when you're on the phone,
Why can't they just leave me alone?
They embarrass you when you're with your friends,
It never ends.

Day after day they're always there for you,
I guess that's fair,
But they're stuck to you!
They are like glue!
They drive me to school,
They help me when I fall,
Although they can be a pest . . .
They'll always be the best!

Isri Kaur Rai (12)
North Leamington School, Leamington Spa

Nonsense

N osy Nora neatly nibbled her nibbly, nasty pasty
O livia loves Ollie's oily, oval olives
N aughty Norris noisily noted his nervous note
S illy Sarah swallowed six super silly sausages
E legant Emily, the elephant, envied Eric, the egg
N aked naturist, Natalie, negatively nested
S uper Simon said 'Supercalifragalisticexpialidocious'
E xcellent Ed ate eight exhilarating eagles.

Emily Forman-Jessop (12)
North Leamington School, Leamington Spa

Lonely Life

Lonely are the nights
Lonely are the days
Lonely am I, in so many ways.

Lonely is the world
Lonely are the seasons
Lonely are the reasons.

Lonely on the land I walk
Lonely on the sea I sail
Lonely in the air I fly
Lonely in the world I stand.

Lonely as I walk along
Lonely school I do attend
Lonely house all on my own
Lonely years are now my friend.

Lonely is my middle name
Lonely is my whole wide world
Lonely is my lifelong aim,
Lonely is what I am.

Jessica Nash (12)
North Leamington School, Leamington Spa

The Description

Loneliness is when someone hasn't got any friends,
Has no one to talk to.

Tearful is when tears roll down your soft, velvety skin,
Or your eyes fill up with sadness.

Gloomy is when the world seems dark and cold,
Like all life has been drained out of the world.

Optimistic is when you expect the best in all worlds.

Positive is when you are free
From doubt or hesitation.

Content is when you feel happy
And fulfilled with your life.

Lauren Cowlishaw (12)
North Leamington School, Leamington Spa

Until I Met You

Before I met you
There were no bubbles in the bath
No leaves on the trees
No love in my heart
And for that we shall never be apart.
Your love led me through my life,
And now we cut our cake with our anniversary knife.
You are the one I love,
Together we fit like a glove.
Before I saw your face
My life was a big disgrace.
I had no idea what to do . . .
Until I met you!

Keris Jones (11)
North Leamington School, Leamington Spa

Lonely

There are millions around me
Yet I feel completely alone.
Their ferocious eyes stare at me
It's not my fault I am different
Their fur is velvety soft
But mine is just dull and dark
They stand, united together
I don't belong here
Sadness is inside me
Sorrow is all around
They are together, never apart
I am an outcast,
With a pain in my heart.

Rebecca O'Connell (12)
North Leamington School, Leamington Spa

Chums

They're for delightful times
Together, for joy and pleasure.

They are there when you need them the most
They never do boast.

Generous, supporting, funny
Almost as sweet and sticky as honey.

Sometimes you find love within them,
Which will stick with you like glue.

That's what real friends are for,
What more could I ask for?

Sebastian Anker-Ryan (12)
North Leamington School, Leamington Spa

Thank You

How brave you are
Giving your life to me;
A seed in your stomach.
A stranger. A mystery.
Before I knew I'd taken it,
I'd uprooted your beautiful heart,
Brought to ruins such strong foundations
Of lifelong dreams. All ripped apart.
You told me to watch my steps,
Yet still I blamed you when I tripped and fell
You rushed to clean the cuts, but couldn't heal the scars
I blamed you for that as well.
Never listening, I was always looking straight through
Stepping on broken glass, swept under the rug.
Ignoring your advice, finding myself. Breaking more glasses.
Pretending not to live each day for one of your hugs
And do you remember your little finger
Wrapped in my soft petal-sized hand?
Please can you lead me back to the photos
I think I lost my way just trying to understand.
The world is tough.
I know somehow I made ours tougher.
Yet you never once turned your back,
But stuck by me, my mother.
Thank you for your love, though I have nothing
To return but my own
I hope it's enough from the disappointment daughter
To know that you'll never find yourself alone
That the love you give, the life you gave
Will never go unknown. Thank you Mum.

Kia Mogg (14)
Penryn College, Penryn

I Woke Up This Morning

I woke up in the morning,
It was raining outside,
So I went to do my paper round,
And nearly cried.
I love her still,
Does she love me?
Let's just talk,
Please listen to me.

You made a mistake,
But don't worry dear,
You shouldn't start to cry,
Because I'm right here,
So hush now baby,
It'll be OK,
Don't worry now,
It won't finish this way.

We need to sort this out,
We need to be together,
Come on now,
Never say never,
We'll make it through,
We always do,
Just trust me
'Cause I love you.

Daniel Hesketh (15)
Penryn College, Penryn

Dr Pepper

Dumb Donald drinks disgusting Dr Pepper
It sizzled like oil in a pan,
And swished from side to side like a man in the sea.
Dripping slowly into his mouth.
I am so tasty,
I'm Dr Pepper.

Josh Amar (12)
Penryn College, Penryn

But Why, How?

Come to the window
See that his dog
Never makes no sound.

We only feel when time
Influences delight.

If man is obscure
She can and will
Ask every question.

By following snow or ice
They then find society
In space but why, how?

With my words
I could and would have said
'Reach and delve through endeavour
And fill up your book
With some form of beauty
And opinion in my character.'

But why, how?

Hayley Dawson (15)
Penryn College, Penryn

Bob

There was a man called Bob
Who liked eating corn on the cob
But once he ran out
And he gave out a shout,
'I need to get more from Rob!'

When Bob went to Rob
He had no corn on the cob
Bob was mad
And wished Rob had
Some more corn on the cob!

Daniel Altenberg (12)
Penryn College, Penryn

I Love You!

You seem to like my mind,
'Cause forever you're inside.
You're more than just a friend,
I'll love you till the end.

Whenever I have cried,
You've stuck by my side,
And when I'm alone,
My heart turns to stone.

But when I see you through the storm,
It makes me feel so warm,
I love you, so very much,
And with every single touch
My eyes turn to yours,
To open all closed doors.

You make my mind float,
You guard me like a moat.
You're more than just a friend,
I'll love you till the end.

Rosie Blindell (12)
Penryn College, Penryn

Dream . . .

Me, you know me, forgotten me but
We've met before
I'm a performance, a lie, a fake, a phoney,
Often when you see me a smile emerges gradually,
But I feel used, undermined, taken for granted,
Without me deathly silences would haunt all of you,
Fear and havoc would reign,
Spine-filling chills all through the night
I love you but at light I am forgotten,
I regret meeting you,
But I'll come back, I promise . . .

Thalia Richardson (12)
Penryn College, Penryn

My Potty Teacher

I have a potty teacher
I'd like you all to know
Her name is Mrs Preacher
OK now off I go!

Her hair is like a bird's nest
Where my chewing gum lies.
She really thinks she's best
Pah! She fills the room with flies!

My teacher Mrs Preacher
Is an absolute nut
She shouldn't be a teacher
Buuuut . . .

My teacher Mrs Preacher
Is absolutely mad
She shouldn't be a teacher
But she's the best we've ever had!

Amy Glover (12)
Penryn College, Penryn

What Shall I Have For Tea Tonight?

As I walk home I start to dream about
Fish and chips with ice cream.

Chicken burgers with Coke and fries
A heap of spaghetti up to your eyes.

Tasty curry, Oreo McFlurry
Super noodles if you're in a hurry.

Chocolate cake and a wafer flake
Roast beef and yucky salad leaves.

What will be for tea for me?
I guess I'll have to wait and see.

Katie Edwards (12)
Penryn College, Penryn

Mystery Man

He's a mystery man that's all he'll ever be
Black coats and soggy clothes
He's a mystery man
To me.

Sneaking around
Day and night
That's all he'll ever do
He might be looking for me
He might be looking for you
Are you a mystery man too?

Jessica Gabriel (12)
Penryn College, Penryn

Football Feelings

I am a football
I keep getting kicked
I really don't like it
And I'm feeling sick.

People keep kicking me
But all I want is a cup of tea,
I'm not very mean
I only wanted to go to the scene
You know what I mean?
I am a football.

Olli Haughton (12)
Penryn College, Penryn

Bugs

B eneath the ground they burrow
U p above they buzz
G ruesome, gorgeous, gleaming, glowing,
S limy like a slug.

Zoe Osmond (12)
Penryn College, Penryn

The Sun

I am light that lightens up your day,
The heat that gives you a tan.

I am hot and shiny,
And if you don't wear suncream you can get burnt.

I am awake at day,
And asleep at night.

I am the glisten in your eyes
I might give you a surprise,
But I can make your day a lot better.

Jake Joyce (12)
Penryn College, Penryn

A Clock

I sit on the wall,
All day, all night, all my life,
Going *tick-tock, tick-tock*
Some people stare at me
Waiting for time to pass,
When I sleep,
People give me a new life,
They turn me to change the time,
Unknown how much it hurts,
I am a clock.

Jodie Hodges (12)
Penryn College, Penryn

The Sun

I am the sun big and bright,
I shine all day but sleep at night.
I'm a ball of fire in the sky
I have to go now, bye-bye!

Katie Walton (11)
Penryn College, Penryn

Grey And White

I am a cloud,
I float around in the sky
Day by day, night by night.
I am a cloud.
Sometimes I am grey, sometimes I am white
And sometimes I only pass by throughout the night.
I am a cloud.
I am fluffy and bright and fly freely in the light.
I am a cloud and I stand proud.

Rosie Louise McGurk (12)
Penryn College, Penryn

The Atmosphere

The sun is as hot as a sizzling sausage
And do I love the sun?
The trees are freckled and so green
And do I love the sun?
Everyone is having fun, running, jumping, jumping and playing.
The beach is all so sunny, happy as can be,
Now I know I'm not the only one who is as happy as can be
And do I love the sun?

Josh Sharp (12)
Penryn College, Penryn

If I Could Fly . . .

If I could fly I would touch the sky.
If I could fly I would wonder why.
If I could fly I would travel far and wide.
If I could fly each cloud would disappear into my eye.
If I could fly I would touch the ocean with my finger
And see my reflection as I go by.
If I could fly I would rescue all living close by.
If you could fly, why oh why can't I?

Matthieu Bethermin (12)
Penryn College, Penryn

My Bike

Shining wheels and brand new chassis
These are things that make me happy
Add them on to my old bike
And it no longer looks like a trike
Take a ride at the jumps
And it breaks like a piece of junk
Now I have to take it to the dumps.

Jake Jones (12)
Penryn College, Penryn

Steep Stone Step

I'm a steep stone step sitting still all day long.
Hay pulled up and down slower and slower every time.
They think I have no feelings, I have no soul,
Now I'm proving them wrong.
I'm strong, I'm hard, they can't push me around.
I do have feelings, I'm a steep stone step.

Tiegan Johns (12)
Penryn College, Penryn

Tick-Tock Clock - Haiku

Tick-tock clock sees all
Tick-tock clock watches us all
Tick-tock clock ticks on.

Wayland Drury (12)
Penryn College, Penryn

Flames - Haiku

Red-hot burning fire
Flames were dancing in the heat
Lovely cake now burnt.

George Sims-Slater (11)
Pontypridd High School, Pontypridd

Fear

I walked to the building with a heavy heart,
My drooping pockets jingling,
I opened the door and the clock bell chimed,
In my head I could hear them ringing.

I stepped forward a few steps,
He was the first thing did I see,
My green eyes glimmered,
I turned around ready to flee.

It was too late I had been spotted,
I was running as fast as I could,
I turned the corner, slipped and fell,
He would catch me soon, I knew he would.

I started to scream, my cry echoing,
My leg lay out in front of me.

Blood squirted at every angle
I couldn't feel it, I could only see.

Tears streamed down my cheeks,
Like a river from my eye,
I waited for this man to come,
In my head I knew I could die.

He was next to me now,
I could smell his sweat,
My heart raced,
Nearly coming out of my chest.

He reached in his pocket and pulled out a gun,
The black plastic shone,
He pulled the trigger with a click and a bang,
One more minute and I was gone.

Hannah Eleri Davies (12)
Pontypridd High School, Pontypridd

My Reality With A Banana Boat

I was on holiday in Africa; Tunisia,
I was lounging on the beach,
The blazing hot sun on my back.

Then I went running into the sea with Sarah.
As I got in I felt the moisture of the clear water.
The sea was very salty,
It stung when the water got into my eyes.

The water had washed in some seaweed,
It got on my nerves, some parts were sharp and hurt,
I wasn't very happy when I got stung by a jellyfish,
It stung like mad.

After that I went on a banana boat,
I was feeling really nervous,
When everyone started to get on I did as well,
When I tried it was so hard,
I eventually got on it, I was at the front.

When it started my heart began to beat faster,
I thought, *what if I fall off, how would I get back on?*
It was going really fast at that moment,
My hands flung back, I had lost grip of the handle,
Luckily my sister was behind me,
She pushed me back,
I was petrified but we didn't turn over,
We just went back and turned over in the shallow end.
I held my nose, I was alive,
I can remember that I was shaken,
I was never going to go on one again.

Farah Iqbal (12)
Pontypridd High School, Pontypridd

No Regret

Trees and flowers so natural
In the summer sun bright and free
Wild and beautiful swaying in the breeze
In the winter snow sleeping soundly

The animals, the river
The little buzzing bees
Grazing and rushing
Fond memories.

But it's time to say goodbye now
The place I know and adore
Is being knocked down, destroyed
To make room for a multistore.

It will soon be overcrowded
And covered in trash
There'll be nothing left to remember
Because it's now a pile of ash.

A horrible sight to see
With smoke covering the air
It's killing our planet
But nobody will care.

I want things back to the way it was
I want to watch the sunrise and set
I want to take a deep breath without coughing
I want no regret.

Cara Sorenti (13)
Pontypridd High School, Pontypridd

Fireworks

Fireworks are so pretty
They're even louder than a kitty
They're all different colours
Like green, blue, yellow and red.

Jemma Reeves (12)
Pontypridd High School, Pontypridd

What On Earth, Is Earth?

What on earth, is Earth?
Are our towns not nature?
We are a part of nature, do our creatures not count?
Where towns stand, nature used to
Are towns a new form of nature?
Monkeys were once the cleverest,
But we evolved,
So can we not say, trees evolved to cities?
What on earth, aren't we doing?
Are we not helping Nature?
We save animals from extinction, present nature,
Should we not do more?
Or should we stop?
We may help, but destruction is human nature.
We may give but not take,
Where luscious forest stood, now lays a tip,
Rat-infested, but what on earth, did we give?
A town, but at the price of what?
Nature's dignity, that's what!
Don't you think we should stop?
We're almost crossed the line!

It's almost too late!

Scott Jenkins (14)
Pontypridd High School, Pontypridd

Stick

One day on the way to school
A stick dropped out of nowhere
It hit me on the head
A stick poem I'm going to say
The stick was cream and brown
Hard and lumpy
Thud as it hit me on the head
It was as hard as a rock.

Mark Hooper (13)
Pontypridd High School, Pontypridd

Get Ready, Get Set, And Go

As they rev it up
And tensions build
They're all set to go,
Helmets hard and goggles tight
All the slots are filled
30 is up and then on its side
Waiting for the light
The light goes red and then yellow
And into gear they flick
The light turns green
And the stands go down
And they're off with one big kick,
Waiting for a winner
Just a few more laps
Adrenaline flowing, heart thumping
Arms aching, legs are stiff
With lips as dry as a desert
It's number 199 who crosses the line first
With the initials TP on his bike and some sponsors covered in mud
He gets the trophy and achievement under his belt
He's making his career big
First place it's Travis Pastrana.

Matthew William Morgan (13)
Pontypridd High School, Pontypridd

Loneliness

I can see nothing
Not even friends.

No one's there
Even for support.
No one's there.

My shadow
My only true friend
I love it.

Matthew Rawlins (13)
Pontypridd High School, Pontypridd

My Poem

P ontypridd High School
O lder people teaching
N aughty children in detention
T ime for break
Y oung people learning
P upils listening
R un through the halls
I love Pontypridd High School, Pontypridd
D on't chew in my classroom
D o your work.

H istory
I CT
G oing home
H olidays!

S chool starts early
C hildren waiting for the bell to go
H ating waking up in the morning
O oh when someone is naughty
O h yeah when the bell goes to go home
L aughing and joking with your best friends.

Leah Emery (12)
Pontypridd High School, Pontypridd

Why Call It Global Warming?

Why is it called Global Warming?
When every day it's snow and storming.
I looked on Google and asked Jeeves
But I still can't get the answer I need.
I asked some people who didn't care
I even tried to phone the mayor
I asked my mum about the question
But all she did was give me a lecture
Finally I got the message of global warming
And I'll try to heed the warning.

Bronwyn Phillips-Griffiths (11)
Pontypridd High School, Pontypridd

Nature Destroyed

The green park where my friends and I used to meet
Has been purely knocked down to make a new street.
The fields in the countryside which is full of cows and horse
Has been turned into an assault course.
There's old things that I've cherished
And the people before me have too
That might be destroyed to make something new.

But sometimes there's a twist to the tale
That the new things they build fail.
Like for example there's an area in my village
which is nearly a swamp,
Forty years ago on that swamp, houses were built,
But before those hoses were sold they began to sink,
And now in the field where those houses used to lie,
Is just rubble, the developers ask why?

Well maybe because the land wasn't right and maybe those problems were all out of sight
So to all of those people who want to destroy something old
To make something new, *think twice.*

Ffion Rowlands (13)
Pontypridd High School, Pontypridd

Watching From A Gondola

My colours are golds and reds to match the magic shirts
I watch from a gondola as the jesters jump around
Looking back and forth as the water is splashing.
I am an old man who's seen many times
The men, women and a toddler or two
Running up and down the roads.
But as many historical figures as there was spaghetti on my Bolognese
I've seen many things
Such wonder to see
But while I sit here some people sing softly.

Kyle Allen (14)
Pontypridd High School, Pontypridd

The Lurking Stranger

I creep through the shadows, not a single soul
Knows I'm there.
It will take skill and pure intelligence
To catch me,
Many have tried, but I don't care.

The things I see and hear when I'm invisible
With the night.
When the day comes along I hide away,
Lurking from the dazzling light.

Dark alleyways and gloomy door frames,
That's where I do my thing.
Selling cheap replicas and stolen goods,
To pay my many loans I owe to the gangster king.

My associates, I keep them close, I like to know what's going on.
I know every dent, scratch and crack around this town,
Every person that's come and gone.

For people's loss I never shed a tear,
When the morning light comes I simply disappear.

Rachel Burrows (12)
Pontypridd High School, Pontypridd

My Room

My bedroom is like a museum,
A pile of dirty washing, a mountain of smelly socks,
Dust bunnies, everywhere, a diary with no key or locks,
My shoes and socks look like my floor,
A sign saying *Beware!* stuck on my door,
All my hats are all over the place,
A pack of cards missing an ace,
Under my bed? Don't get me started!
It actually smells like someone has farted!
My bedroom looked like this on the 1st May,
But don't worry, I cleaned it yesterday!

Cora Nott (12)
Pontypridd High School, Pontypridd

Memories

On where, of which, I swung as a child,
On where, of which, my memories piled.
I thought they'd keep stacking up and up,
But suddenly appeared a big hiccup.

It devastated me right to the heart,
Knowing that I couldn't play in my park.

Because something manmade took over it,
I wish I could sort that split,
Between me and my swinging friends,
But I can't help that, it's now the end.

I used to swing high on that swing every day,
Rush my dinner and run away,
The bond I had with my park,
Was like the ocean and a shark.

I'd love to know why it got replaced,
Love to know why it got defaced.

My park.

Natasha Hill (14)
Pontypridd High School, Pontypridd

Untitled

Stars in the sky
Sparkle in my eye.

The moon way up high
Planes flying by.

Shooting stars zooming past
Just hold that thought as long as it lasts.

Rockets zoom up into space,
Just to see the look on your face.

UFOs and aliens too
What else? No one knows apart from you!

Dani Jones (13)
Pontypridd High School, Pontypridd

Why Poem

Why is she tall?
Why is she funny?
Why is she loud?
Why is she pretty?

Why does she cry?
Why does she smile?
Why does she laugh?
Why does she wonder?

Why can she touch?
Why can she smell?
Why can she hear?
Why can she see?

Why is she right?
Why is she wrong
Why is she here?
Why, oh, why, oh why?

Chloe Hooper (12)
Pontypridd High School, Pontypridd

The Stick

The stick has lots of shades of brown
Like muddy water
Like in the sea on a rainy day.

The bark is rough like the back of a crocodile
Which is sleeping in the open air.

I drop it
And drop it on my hard table
To see if it is tough like a boxer on form.

It has lumps and bumps
Like on the beach
Relaxing calmly
With the sun gazing down on it.

Ian Kelland (14)
Pontypridd High School, Pontypridd

My Why Poem!

Why is the sky blue, Mam?
Why are their tall and small people?
Why is there always someone in a pub, Mam?
Why can't I go in a pub like other people?

Why is there clouds in the sky, Mam?
Why doesn't rabbits make a sound?
Why are some people that like green, Mam?
Why am I asking these questions?

Why are boys so annoying, Mam?
Why is mud brown?
Why do people like pizzas, Mam?
Why do I have to wear long johns?

Why do people have long hair, Mam?
Why do people like television?
Why do people have blonde hair, Mam?
Why do dogs have good vision?

Samantha Thomas (12)
Pontypridd High School, Pontypridd

Friends!

Friends will help you
Through the good and bad
They'll stay by your side
Through moments happy and sad

I know I can trust you
I know you'll be there
I know you've a friend that's
Loving and cares.

Through all the wrongs and all the rights,
I'm here for you, to be a
Best friend that's true.

'Cause I love you and that's what BFs do.

Chloe Lee Willetts (13)
Pontypridd High School, Pontypridd

Why Nan, Why?

Why is your hair grey, Nan?
Why do you always stroke the cat?
Why do you always say hey, Nan?
Why do you always wear that stupid hat?

Why can't you do what we can, Nan?
Why do your eyes look like roses?
Why do you look at that man, Nan?
Why do we smell out of our noses?

Why do you always wear that skirt, Nan?
Why don't you wear slippers?
Why do you drag mud in the house, Nan?
Why do you wear such long knickers?

Why do you always have that hair dye, Nan?
Why don't you like pink?
Why do you wear them shoes, Nan?
Why do you write with ink?

Hannah Lee (12)
Pontypridd High School, Pontypridd

Nothing Mattered

The trees blew
The monkeys chattered
The flowers grew
Everything mattered.

The children played
The mothers nattered
The swing swayed
Everything mattered.

The trees are gone
The parks battered
It feels so wrong
Nothing mattered.

Carter Langford (14)
Pontypridd High School, Pontypridd

A Twig

A twig is a stick insect
Camouflaged against all types of materials
A twig is a bristle, solid
Connected to a hundred-year-old tree.

A twig is a fragile piece
Of the world
Important in every way.

A twig is a mixture
Of brown paint
Exploded all over it
In different ways.

A twig sways
In the cold winter breeze
Covered in a coat of icicles
Waiting and crying, wishing
Winter would never return.

Jessica Davies (14)
Pontypridd High School, Pontypridd

What Have We Done?

The forest has gone,
There are no trees left,
But we have to move on,
And protect all the rest.

Now there are new homes,
Making pollution even bigger,
The only nature left here is stones,
Why are we not taking enough caution?

That old field is now a site for a digger,
And the old orange tree is now a house,
Pollution keeps getting bigger,
Soon there won't even be a home for a poor little mouse.

Thomas Morris (14)
Pontypridd High School, Pontypridd

Why?

Why do lions run, Dad?
Why do teachers bore?
Why can't I look at the sun, Dad?
Why does two and two equal four?

Why are you falling asleep, Dad?
Why does everyone eat?
Why is the swimming pool deep, Dad?
Why can't you fit in your seat?

Why do kids play, Dad?
Why don't you answer?
Why should we go to school on Friday, Dad?
Why am I a terrible dancer?

Why do birds fly, Dad?
Why do fish swim?
Why do kids keep asking why, Dad?
Why are you so dim?

Daniel William Jones (11)
Pontypridd High School, Pontypridd

Before All This

Cars beeping, gas leaking,
Traffic producing puffs of smoke,
Light gleaming, traffic cheating,
All that's left are swings that are broke.

Trucks popping, wheels bopping,
Lorries chugging along an open road.
Traffic polluting, cars hooting,
A squashed animal, this used to be a toad.

Before all this, there used to be fields,
There used to be forestry and animals.
Before all this, there used to be beauty,
It will never be the same again.

Rhiannon Wattley (13)
Pontypridd High School, Pontypridd

Why Poem!

Why is the grass green?
Why do the ducks like the pond, Dad?
Why is my friend called Bean?
Why are pigs pink, Dad?

Why are some people relaxed?
Why is the sea blue, Dad?
Why do you pay tax?
Why do we need to go to school, Dad?

Why is chocolate brown?
Why are people famous, Dad?
Why do you give me a frown?
Why are you so big, Dad?

Why is my cousin called Ned?
Why is Mam blonde, Dad?
Why do I love my bed?
Why is the world round, Dad?

Zac Byard (12)
Pontypridd High School, Pontypridd

My Why Dad? Poem

Why are there leaves on trees, Dad?
Why is the grass green, Dad?
Why will Gran have to leave, Dad?
Why are you going bald?

Why has your dad got a beard, Dad?
Why do you need to be quiet, Dad?
Why did you bleed, Dad?
Why are you showing your teeth?

Why have I got all these questions?
Why won't you answer them all?
Why won't you answer my questions?
Why have you taken my ball?

Jennifer Bohen (12)
Pontypridd High School, Pontypridd

The Twig

The twig looks like thin liquorice
Hanging from the sky.

Fallen to the ground
When it's ready to eat.

The twig smells like morning dew on the ground,
Lying there lonely
Waiting to be found.

The twig flees like bumpy stones
On a wall
Waiting to be ready
So they can fall.

The twig sounds like Rice Krispies
Erupting in a bowl.
Staying there until they get old.

Hollie Jones (14)
Pontypridd High School, Pontypridd

Dan-Y-Cribyn

It used to be so quiet and peaceful,
Hearing happy children play all day.

Seeing people walk by with their dogs
Being so friendly.

But then things started to change,
As they got taken away.

Now it ain't so quiet and peaceful,
But loud cars booming up the street.

People being so friendly turn into youngsters smoking,
Drinking and swearing.

But as I look out of my window
I see my environment was full of nature,
Now it's full of pollution!

Karly Samuel (14)
Pontypridd High School, Pontypridd

Fading Beauty

Her hair was glistening like a lake
The smell of roses all around
What once was beauty now is fake
But her voice is still a lovely sound

She does not care who she hurts
But they all follow to her delight
She dresses up in short cut skirts
And skintight dresses in the night

It doesn't matter, not to her
'Why should I care?' is what she'll say
She drowns her sins in her liquor
And she's always got at least one ashtray

But in some ways I feel sorry and sad
Because she didn't live the life that's she could've once had.

Holly Rebecca Simmons (12)
Pontypridd High School, Pontypridd

Why?

Why do birds suddenly appear, Roxy?
Why do frogs leap high in the sky?
Why do monkeys swing from tree to tree?
Why do people have pets, Roxy?

Why do people use technology, Roxy?
Why do trees grow?
Why do flowers grow colourful
Why do chickens lay eggs, Roxy.

Why do people ride bikes, Roxy?
Why do people eat?
Why do people have to work
Why do we have teachers, Roxy?

Why, why, why,
   Roxy?

Carys Ashcroft (12)
Pontypridd High School, Pontypridd

The London Blitz

The sun was shining down on London, warming the ground
There was a drone, which seemed to get very loud
Planes appeared flying very low
Everything seemed to happen very slow
Bombs started to fall without warning
People were running and shouting
Black smoke rose into the sky, engulfing the light
Suddenly the day seemed to turn to night
With every bomb the ground shook and buildings seemed to disappear
People stood in the streets, their eyes full of tears.
Others tried to put fires out or were helping.
It was like the world was ending.
What had we done wrong?
All hope was gone.

Matthew Lacey (13)
Pontypridd High School, Pontypridd

The Tump

A large green mountain where children would play,
Back in the day, people would say.
All the flowers, trees, stringy green grass,
Hours of happiness, hours that last.
Until one day all had gone,
The happiness, laughter, cheerful songs.
Now, big brown blocks, with roofs and chimneys,
Replace what once were large green trees.
Different emotions come from this day,
Where all memories of that mountain were washed away.
Some happy, because of their new humble abode,
Some saddened as the memories slowed.
Will the mountain ever return?
Will the big brown blocks ever move?
No one knows.

Amy-Jane Davies (14)
Pontypridd High School, Pontypridd

Time To Beat

Drummers are the timekeepers with all their beats,
Rhythms, splashes and crashes,
They are always tapping!
Whether it is rock, jazz, blues or samba
They always keep in time.

People have drummed for thousands of years.
The beat makes people happy.
They played on wooden drums with animal skins,
Now people play on huge kits with lots of cymbals to clash.

People like the drums because the beat makes them feel good,
It's catchy and infectious.
You will never forget the rhythm; it's like it is drummed into your head.
Every time you play you learn a little bit more.

James Hoey (13)
Pontypridd High School, Pontypridd

Is Our World Changing?

What is our world without love,
Its foggy air from up above.
Trees have been devastated with deforestation
And ruined for our generation.
Rain falls drop by drop,
It comes when it comes and stops when it stops.
The fresh air that Mother Nature provides,
It separates the outdoors from the inside.
To make sure our world survives,
Let's keep up and devise,
A plan of action now and today,
To change tomorrow in a better way.
People who claim to love the Earth,
Should learn to respect it for its own worth.

Rebecca Williams (13)
Pontypridd High School, Pontypridd

Say Hello To Goodbye

Well, well, well here we are again
The beginning of the tragic end.
There's nothing left worth saving
Soon the world will start caving.

Lost every ounce of hope locked deep inside
Time to find a place to run and hide.
Taking short cuts and false illusions
Just to find a much easier solution.

Bitter heart pumping blood around my veins
Nothing but a tin man I don't feel any pain.
Hypocrites and liars stand right before our eyes.
Going to remain slaves for the rest of our lives.

Rachael Parr (14)
Pontypridd High School, Pontypridd

Why?

Why is water wet, Mum?
Why have zebras got stripes?
Why are cheetahs so fast, Mum?
Why are stars so bright?

Why does ice melt, Mum?
Why do babies cry?
Why do we sleep all night, Mum?
Why do we say goodbye?

Why do birds sing, Mum?
Why do parrots talk?
Why do people work, Mum?
Why can't babies walk?

Paige Pritchard (11)
Pontypridd High School, Pontypridd

I'm Really Sorry, Sir . . .

'Where is your homework, boy?'

'I can explain, Sir . . .

My dad was hungry
My mom took it to work
I dropped it down the drain
It fell out of my pocket, Sir.

My cat missed the litter box
I was rushing and forgot it
My mum recycled it
It fell down the toilet as I was checking it, Sir.

    I'm really sorry, Sir . . .'

Rhys Goodwin (12)
Pontypridd High School, Pontypridd

Fear

Fear is fear
Fear is the roaring flames from the burning Hell.
Fear is the anger and revenge that you cannot resist.
Fear is the sight of a malicious grin of an angered devil's face.
Fear is the thought of terrifying death.
Fear is the coldness of a pitch-black night.
Fear is the sound of a cry at night.
Fear is the touch of cold, dark blood.
Fear is the old creepy clock striking midnight.
Fear is the thought of an old spooky man following you at night.
Fear is all around us.
Fear is fear!

Thomas Ashton (14)
Pontypridd High School, Pontypridd

Nature

What is nature?
Nature is the beautiful scenery,
An invisible spirit.

It's quiet with the smallest creatures passing through
But also dominated by the beasts of the Earth.

It's something that can give life
But also take it ferociously.

We should not mess with this,
Or eventually it will mess
With us.

Luke Price (14)
Pontypridd High School, Pontypridd

When Walking In The Woods One Day

When walking in the woods one day,
I stepped upon a twig,
The twig went snap and I stepped back.

Down I bent to pick it up
And felt its shape so rough and round
When I looked there were lots of others on the ground.

I walked along and started to chew
This little twig of mine
Its taste was one I did not like
So threw it to the sky.

Jarrod Evans (13)
Pontypridd High School, Pontypridd

Our World

Stand back, and watch the world crumble
All you can hear is engineering's rumble
The place you used to know is now a concrete jungle.

Soon everything will be gone; the plants, the trees
Can't you hear Mother Nature's screaming pleas?
Even the children are begging on their knees!

We are pumping pollution into the air and the sea
Can't you understand that this shouldn't be?
Now the Earth is just a spinning heap of debris.

Emily Pardoe (14)
Pontypridd High School, Pontypridd

Gone Now

The trees have gone now
They've been cut down for paper
Why are we doing this? Is it just a caper?

The little old park has gone now
It's been flattened to make room for homes
We're killing our world, can you hear its groans?

The clean air has gone now
Factories, aerosols and fumes
Why don't we fight to stop the polluting smoke plumes?

Lucy Watts (14)
Pontypridd High School, Pontypridd

Crazy Baby!

There once was a baby,
She seemed a little bit crazy
She sat in her chair
Pulling her last strands of hair
And now she's getting quite lazy!

Kate Taylor (12)
Pontypridd High School, Pontypridd

The Leaf

The leaf blows in the wind
And changes colour in the autumn,
Blooming with its beautiful colours.

The leaf falls from the tree,
Softly landing to the ground
By the side of a bee.

The leaf is a wonderful green
With a million of the other leaves,
They form a team.

Amy Bishop (13)
Pontypridd High School, Pontypridd

Twig

The twig is as long and thin as a lace.
The lace is hard and brown.

The twig feels rough, hard like sandpaper
And as flaky as cornflakes.

The twig sounds crackly like an untouched floor of white snow
Being stepped on.

A twig smells like sap from the bark
That has been ripped off the twig.

Mathieu Austin (14)
Pontypridd High School, Pontypridd

Love

Love is a pink blossom,
It feels like a fluffy spring bunny
Love tastes like freshly made pink candyfloss
It smells like a sweet pink rose
It sounds like a bird singing a lovely song
Love lives on a beautiful clear white cloud!

Teigan Jones (12)
Pontypridd High School, Pontypridd

A Cold Summer's Morning

As I stepped out into a cold summer's morning
I found the log
The log smelt rotten and looked like a crunchie
Listen you'll hear the leaves all around
It's prickly, green and came from a tree
Soft to the inner touch
Spiky to the outer.

Morgan Bowen (14)
Pontypridd High School, Pontypridd

My White Night - Haikus

On a frosty night
The ground is covered in white
People slip with fright.

Now I need some light
I want to go for a bite
I need some delight.

Aimee Louise Morris (12)
Pontypridd High School, Pontypridd

I Am A Boy

I am a boy that loves to play
Especially in the day.
I am a boy that loves to say
I have fun every day.
I am a boy that loves to climb
Even though falling hearts for a while.

Jake Barlow (12)
Pontypridd High School, Pontypridd

The Young Fools

Who do they think they are
The young fools
To treat other people badly, answer people back
And gladly sit around all day?
Smoking and getting drunk 'cause they think it's cool
But they don't know what they're doing to themselves
The fools.

Going out, causing trouble,
Standing around in a big huddle
Shouting, screaming, causing sleepless nights,
Starting stupid, pointless fights
Ruining their future, threatening to kill
The ones they love.
They come closer to you and push and shove.
You scurry off home,
Make sure they're not following,
Making sure you're alone.

And in the morning when they wake up,
Not remembering the times that they threw up
Their heads are banging from the inside,
Last night washes over them like the tide.

Then they remember the chaos they caused,
Now there's nowhere to run, nowhere to hide.
People are out there waiting to get them
Get them sorted,
Teach them a lesson.

Hannah McCrory (13)
Poole High School, Poole

The Lonely Moon

The large round sphere
That sits in the sky.
A large globe of light,
That accompanies Earth at night.
He sits there in nothingness,
But what is he there for and why?

Surrounded by plenty of stars,
But he daren't go near their light.
Just floating by Earth
Disappearing by day,
And glowing distinctly by night.

His great white shine
Provides us with romantic evenings.
He is the pleasant nightlight in space.
Children look up to him from their bedroom window,
And admire his white featured face.

We humans we have visited him before,
The moon does get lonely once in a while,
So we send our astronauts.
The personality of the moon is extremely pleasant,
And sometimes when he gets bored of his looks,
He changes into a crescent!

Ellie Parr (13)
Poole High School, Poole

Song Of The Free Range Hen

I hate where I live.
I walk on the grass all day, it's always wet.
It makes me cold and hurts my feet.
I feel terrible,
I feel the breeze,
But it only makes me feel colder.
The sun glares at me
But it holds no warmth.

You can come see me if you want,
I'm the one with brown feathers and white wing tips.
You won't have to look for long,
There are not many of us, it's lonely,
I'm also the quietest.
Most of us keep quiet, we don't have much to say,
I usually stay in the middle, alone.

I'm anxious of the hens in the shelter,
They can talk to each other
And always share companions.
I've never been in there, but I'm sure it's pleasant,
It's always so loud,
I wish I was with them,
I'm so alone.

Graham Rigler (14)
Poole High School, Poole

The Young Fools

Why do they think this has happened, the young fools?
What's made them like this?
Do they somehow suppose that it is more grown up to shout instead of talk?
And to throw abuse or use bad language as soon as someone so much as looks at them?
If they choose to terrorise an old woman on the way back from her weekly shop,
Throwing rocks and stones and laughing if someone tried to help her?
Or do they fancy knocking down a neighbour's bin every time they walk past?
Or sit for days on end watching the TV screen?
In life you make up the parts of you
You start speeding up in age and can never go back to what you've done.

Every day you meet new people and every moment you should cherish
Before you know it you're a teenager, your attitude shows it's coming.
Loud-mouthed, back chatting and a face filled with mountains of pus.
Show's you're in for it!

Lauren Nicolson (14)
Poole High School, Poole

Volcano

Volcano, she is one you will soon recognise,
She is filled with deep surprise.
When frustrated her rage shows with her radiant red glow,
Down her body the molten tears flow.
Soon everyone will realise they're in danger from the anger she has begun to show.
From the emotions she expressed it is not hard to see she is troubled,
As every second the danger is doubled.

So fuming she screams and begins to steam,
When this happens everyone is sure to be wiped out clean.
She becomes angered and aggressive even more.
This is when she cannot take it anymore
And trembles to the ground.

After the commotion she becomes extremely tired,
Some say this is when she is most admired.
This is because she is now peaceful and calm
Nobody will she now harm.

Volcano, some would say she is beautiful at rest,
But I think when expressive she looks her best!

Danni Peart (13)
Poole High School, Poole

Volcano!

As one temperature rises
The volcano starts to dribble,
Begins to lose control.
Nature tries to soothe his throat,
Then heartburn strikes
He starts to cough up blood,
Which stains the land,
Leaving scars on his body.
He cannot move.
He can only wait for help.
His life is long, painful and hot.
Just waiting for his life to end,
But if he waits and holds it in he will explode.
He won't die, just wait in pain.
What did he do to deserve this?
But when he dies his body will remain
Blood still boiling.
Anger still raging but his soul gone
Just a lifeless rock causing destruction.

Dann Cobb (14)
Poole High School, Poole

The Moon

The moon with his cold marble
Face lights up the night sky,
Looking after the bright stars,
As father of the night.

We gaze upon him as he glows,
Upon us, acting so proud,
Even if he's covered by clouds.

He circles the world with his airs
And graces
And has so many changing faces.

Stacey Ayling (14)
Poole High School, Poole

The Moon

A gateway to space for all, spacecraft,
The lens of a gargantuan torch, lighting up the night sky.
A child's night light, comforting them as they go to sleep,
A werewolf's signal for its howl.
A cheesy planet for the mice,
A surface like sandpaper, rough and bumpy.
Immense craters like the tops of volcanoes,
Towering rocks like skyscrapers crowded across its surface.
A colossal football floating around.
Earth's little brother,
Always staying close.
The king of Earth checking up on us at the end of each day.
The moon is on guard for any comets or meteors.
A sign for aliens,
It keeps a close eye, watching Earth to see what's happening.
It races around Earth, giving light to each country at night,
A sparkly jewel twinkling in the night sky.
This is Earth's moon!

Liam Jerrett (14)
Poole High School, Poole

The Moon

Silvery-white, like a wise old man
You've been here from the dawn of time
Your face so high, shining onto us
The grandfather we all know, love and trust.

Glowing and smiling like an innocent child
Playing with the stars in the fields of space
Peeking out from behind the covers of darkness
To light up the sky with your cheeky grin.

Warming and soothing like a mother's embrace
Protecting and guiding and welcoming home
All of the sailors like long-lost sons
Lighting the way home with your wisdom and grace.

Rebecca Phillips (13)
Poole High School, Poole

The Young Fools

Why do you think they act like that?
What do you think inspires them
To pursue their idol interests?
What do you think has made them like this?
Do they presume it's grown up to scream and shout?
Do they enjoy being the top dog, the king?
Do they like to be feared by children half their size
Do they think they're hard, solid, strong?
Do they know they're ignorant, stupid and idle?
Do they know or are they all fools?

Why do they act confident when they are scared of themselves, each other?
They are stupid, short-haired, baggy-clothed morons.
They should appreciate what they have while they have it.
They should be kind to those who will employ them
And not push them in toilets because although the teenagers forget
The little 'runts' won't.

Robert Smith (13)
Poole High School, Poole

The Moon

Here I am, up and alone
Looking down on you
Happiness and sadness are what I see
While children sing in my light
I sit here shimmering on you
While your smile makes my night
Making me shimmer at best
I wish I could feel love and hate
I wish I wasn't alone up here
But I guess this is my life
With all of the stars and planets
Shining over you.

Hollie Brunyee (13)
Poole High School, Poole

Song Of The Free Range Hen

Where's my food, I want it now!
If you want an egg then I have to be fed.
I'm royalty to all you cluckers.

I suppose I get it quite good,
I'm allowed to go outside
And I'm not cooped up in a cage
And fighting for something to eat.

I have good friends right until the end
At least I know what's out there
I'm not alone and my eggs are worth a lot
Which means I gain better food and amazing treatment.

I wish one day the rest of my kind will be able to live as I do
This is because it is unfair that they are the same as I.
Why are they treated so appallingly?
And nobody, not even you, can be bothered to notice them.

Ryan Stiggants (13)
Poole High School, Poole

Gritted Teeth

Space probes constantly passing by,
Blocking her view.
Casting shadows of technology,
Over her infuriated scowl.
At first she understood, humans were young,
She sighed at their ignorance and lay back in her bed of stars.
Yet their ignorance blinded their respect, and blinded her sight.
Then she was alone, forever dark, forever alone,
Cursed by the ignorance of humanity
Yet could do nothing, but grit her teeth.

William Clayton (14)
Poole High School, Poole

The Volcano

The volcano trembled and shook,
Licked his lips,
Tasting the fear rushing out of his victims,
With one huge roar he threw up the lava,
Unleashing it upon his prey.
Launched it out again and again,
Roar after roar, seeing the people suffer,
Watching them run with fear.
And with one last shudder,
Unleashed an almighty explosion,
Of lava and ash covering the surroundings,
Destroyed its beauty and ruined lives with it.
He chuckled to himself.
Then prepared to sleep once again,
Ready to claim more victims next time!

Fraser Moors (14)
Poole High School, Poole

The Young Fools

What are they thinking, the young fools,
To make them do this?
Do they assume it's more grown up to 'hang about' and 'be cool'
And keep running away, when the police drive past
For reports of smashing, stealing and sparring?
Or that they're scared
Of being on the other end of the stick
Getting bullied, being pushed around?
Or do they do it for fun
And have they always been 'hanging out'?
Menacing on the street corners, waiting for something that will never come.
Just stalking as the world goes by.
Always wanting fun,
Why don't they go out and find some?

Josh Kitching (13)
Poole High School, Poole

Young Fools

They cloak themselves.
Hooded and wary, frightened souls,
Ready to scare off their rivals,
Screaming, uproaring, ready to prove they're worthy
Of the girl or lad they desire,
Sharpened tools to scare off foes.

The streets crowded after dark,
Corners lit only by cigarette butts,
Along with piercing tools used for thrills,
Wet, rubbery cases cast away in bushes.

Infants raised by benefits
Lights flashing, raving parties,
Oh these people have no idea,
Of the future yet to come.

Zachary Beavan (14)
Poole High School, Poole

A Cat's Nine Lives

Cats have nine lives,
Mine lost five, but I gave them back
As a present from me,
I gave one back by playing with my cat,
She got one back by being cheeky and a little sneaky,
She got the rest back by being a cat, you know what cats do,
They play and eat and sleep a little too,
Now my cat has nine lives,
The shine's back in her eye (I don't know why)
Now the miaow makes me smile,
She has all her lives now and is doing what cats do,
Playing and eating and sleeping a little too!

Amy Cooper (12)
Redland Green School, Bristol

Holes

The blood dries in my cracking veins,
A sense of paranoia as I gaze across the plain,
A sudden flood of memory as I stare up to the sun,
I start to wonder, am I still sane?
And I keep digging on.

Left for dead would be a slight exaggeration,
My head stays straight as I focus my fixation,
A sudden flood of memory as I stare up to the sun,
My canteen taunting me with an open invitation,
And I keep digging on.

Mouth so dry it mimics the ground,
I move my lips but I hear no sound,
A sudden flood of memory as I stare up to the sun,
I see them watching, but there's no one around,
And I keep digging on.

Heart that's dancing, awaits a prayer,
They won't give in, they leave me there,
A sudden flood of memory as I stare up to the sun,
A cross of a line, hear the paper tear,
And I keep digging on.

The blood dries in my cracking veins,
A sense of paranoia as I gaze across the plain,
A sudden flood of memory as I stare up to the sun,
I start to wonder, am I still sane?
And I keep digging on.
And I keep digging on.

Aelliey Kelly (13)
Redland Green School, Bristol

Reflected Feelings

Waiting at the port of Dover
For the ship to take me to war
I want it to be all over
So I don't have to see much gore

A big transport plane touches down
This is my ticket to battle
I am so scared I start to frown
And all my teeth start to rattle

All walking on the upper deck
Coughing, chatting and being scared
We all look like a complete wreck
Shoes all sodden but none of us cared

In my seat I start to cower
Ring, ring, ring, ring, there goes the bell
Seat belts on, soon it is the hour
When everyone walks into Hell

Marching all the way to the front
I really know this won't be fun
Oh no, my bayonet is blunt
Damn! I need it to fight the Hun

Musa Qaleh is where I'll go
Where I'll spend all my nights
Each hour so painfully slow
And I know I will have some frights

We are waiting in the trenches
Writing messages to loved ones
Our sectors full of stenches
And people wounded making groans

Lying in my regiment's tent
I am thinking of months to come
I'm wanting to go home to Kent
Where I can be safe and see Mum

About to go over the top
Out there, God will be my best friend
All the dangers, I start to drop
I can't begin to comprehend

Our sector's on a patrol
To try and stop the Taliban
Out here everything's so unnatural
And this was started by one man

There goes the whistle, we charge out
To no-man's-land, the stench of flesh
Many death cries, screams and a shout
The smell of blood, so very fresh

Walking along, chatting to Kirt
Bang! The firing of a mortar
We all jump down and hit the dirt
But still leading to more slaughter

Crack! Then I feel pain in my thighs
And there is a blood-searing burn
All my life flashes before my eyes
No war, when will they ever learn?

I try to get to cover, *boom!*
And there is a blood-searing burn
Death! That feeling starts to loom
No war, when will we ever learn?

Max Heiberg-Gibbons (13)
Redland Green School, Bristol

The Reflection

I was waiting for purr-fection
When you walked through that puddle,
I saw your furry reflection
And then got in a big muddle.

Behind you was a building
That was as red as fire,
And now the poem is unfolding,
I read it with much desire.

You were a skinny little chap
And weren't very small,
You didn't sit on my lap,
But walked straight to the wall.

I don't know where you'd been,
I don't know if you had a home,
But I know you'd been seen,
'Cause they saw you in 'The Dome'.

Your fur was clean but colourful,
You were as fragile as a butterfly,
I thought you looked wonderful,
So stopped you from walking by.

The sun shone on the rooftops
Making them glimmer in the light,
Reminding me of the fizzy pops
That I ate before the fight.

You lay there eating fries,
Until I noticed whose you were
And started to make up the lies
To save your dainty little paws.

The puddle was as blue as the sky,
As blue as the van outside
And then you miaowed 'goodbye'
And went off to hide.

When you went I saw something good,
'Twas a bit of paper on the post
Saying, 'Find this black cat, and keep it'
So that was when I realised it was you!

Hannah Crook (11)
Redland Green School, Bristol

The Forgotten Park

Deserted, unloved!
The park was once a place of happiness, memories and fun.
Now it is, or seems to be,
One of those places you never want to see.
The swings are rusty and old
And the sandpit is far from 'sandy',
The fence is covered in graffiti
And the slide is ultra dirty.
The only people who go there
Are the boys in big black hoodies.

The park is full of litter
From those few who go there.
The green grass is far too long,
But nobody seems to care,
Not that I'm aware.

Dust covers the weedy path,
A plastic bin is at one side,
Full to the top with waste,
Creating an overwhelming stench.
So very bad it scares away
Those little kids coming to play!

Even though it doesn't sound great,
At least there is this sort of place
Where kids can come
And have some fun!
This is the park . . .

Isobel Pickering (11)
Redland Green School, Bristol

The Ballad Of The Eco-Home

'Tell us the story Grandpa
Of how you saved our home,
And about the silly neighbours
Who always had to moan!'

'Well, the silly neighbours
Came round and did protest,
I tried and tried to reason with them
And then they did suggest:

'Dear Mr Neville,
We just don't like your plans
You might be good at football
But we're not your biggest fans

The house will be an eyesore,
An embarrassment to us all,
With its football hedge and stupid shape
It's not what we'd call cool.'

The reply they got from Gary
Was not what they'd expect,
'I want to save the planet!'
Which left them quite perplexed.

They changed their minds quite quickly
And came to see his view,
They even helped him build it,
And now it's here for you.'

Barnaby Mather (13)
Redland Green School, Bristol

Elephants Are Cool

Elephants are cool,
They charge around and rule,
They run up and down,
Get covered in mud, and are brown.

Underwater they laugh and chortle,
Using their trunk as a snorkel,
Paddling everywhere,
Without a single care.

They carry people around,
Then never fall down,
Weaving through the trees,
Stepping over the crumpled leaves.

They love to eat some buns
And go for walks and runs,
They are ever so tall,
But never look a fool.

They're scared of only two things,
But otherwise they are like kings,
These things are ants and humans,
That wear their terrible plumes.

That is why they're cool
And they really do rule.

Annie Allen (11)
Redland Green School, Bristol

Holes

A relentless sun penetrates the hills on an enduring horizon,
Weary campers struggle to continue.
Waves of heat pry up from the ground.
Frightening blankets of confining sand cover the barren wasteland.

Ferocious creatures leap from soldier to soldier
Inflicting excruciating pain to any that come across them.
The scorching expanse controlled by death and destruction;
Powerful killers, dangerously fight to demise.

A bleak desert dawns upon the enclosed fear.
Blistering wind hurtles towards the unsuspecting victim;
Nothing, for miles around.
Just sand.
Water is terminating for the consuming victims.

Pain envelopes the strugglers as they believe their time is near.
Their expressive hands are covered in blisters;
Minds are packed with the notion of emptiness,
As emotions scuttle wild and free.

Campers scream for attention;
But the internees are feral.
They will not return to them now.
Lost.
Not one more will dig holes.

Elliot Sandammeer Brewer (12)
Redland Green School, Bristol

Jabberywocky 2
(Based on 'The Jabberwocky' by Lewis Carrol)

'Twas dark and the rotten trees
Did crack and crumble in the wind,
All timid were the frumpy bees
And the squirrel babies grinned.

I heard a squelch in the mud
Among the deserted ground,
A heavy thud filled the air
A horrible, chilling sound.

The silhouetted something
Came towards them with a thud,
'Twas gulingthing and gulumthing
As it was splashing in the mud.

Its feet fulumpled
As it waddled through the trees
Its round belly rumbled
Disturbing the whisper of the breeze.

Its eye caught a baboo
As it stepped towards it slowly
'I found you!'
It said to its good friend Rolly.

Sophie Back (11)
Redland Green School, Bristol

Young And Ill

I see her cry,
I see her weep,
Will she die?
Will she sleep?
Her pain,
Her sorrow,
No gain,
No tomorrow,
Her life,
Her fears,
Her strife,
Her tears,
The illness beckons her
To her death.

Am I dead?
Or am I living?
Shall I keep on giving?
Or shall I take away?
My life,
My tears,
In all these years
That started one sunny day.

Rachel Perry-Watts (12)
Redland Green School, Bristol

Old People

They listen with dignity and then they say,
'So, what's the latest today?'
We reply with another gadget that means nothing to them,
They just smile and say, 'Hem, hem!'

Then when we've gone they get up and say,
'What on earth? What is it? They've lost their way?'
They go to bed muttering, full of ideas
About young people and their peers.

They read the morning news with much clucking
'All these children are really bucking
With the weight of all their crimes.'

But who are they to say?
Surely there was crime in their days!
Some have tried to be good and failed,
Some have even been put on bail.

So here is the question,
The one big thing -
Whose fault?
Who's turn?
Where to go?

Saskia Wootton-Cane (11)
Redland Green School, Bristol

Peace (My Point Of View)

All of the fighting,
All of the war,
All of the people can't try no more,
Why don't we just give it a rest?
At least I know I'm doing my best.
As much as I try, as much as I plead
It doesn't seem to help people's needs.
With all of the suffering, with all of the pain.
What do all the other folks gain?

It's not my fault, it's not my sin.
I wasn't the person to begin.
When people cry, when people shout
I want to go over there and help them out!
I want love, I want peace.
If the sign was on my hoodie there would be a crease.
I wish people helped, I wish people cared.
Instead people just stand there and stare.

How can I help, what can I do?
It seems like it's down to just me and you!

Tallulah Clark (12)
Redland Green School, Bristol

My Xbox

Happy, scared, excited
These are the emotions I get
When I play on my Xbox.

Playing against other people even on the net . . .
The picture getting better
But sometimes getting worse . . .

The only thing keeping me going is
Knowing that the excitement won't ever end . . .

This is what I think when I play on my Xbox.

Isaac Williams (12)
Redland Green School, Bristol

Holes Poem

Picture this,
A barren-like wasteland,
Empty and bare,
You're stranded and lost,
But does anyone care?
So hot in the day,
Yet cold in the night,
Just hope someone finds me,
If only, if only.

Why did I come here,
This torturous place?
So hostile,
The sun convulsing my face,
When every single step you take
Blisters your feet
Until they ache,
Imagine if I got back,
Wouldn't that be great?
If only, if only.

Cameron Merchant (13)
Redland Green School, Bristol

Lisheng Roomclass
(Inspired by 'The Jabberwocky' by Lewis Carrol)

The madaflom bimbleings were dreadful things.
Every flyzoz could not slip.
For the zipadangs came up nizly-tong with icky frams on their dip.

'By nost go fliba flabjab, or rasta gets a bloon.
If every flyzoz does a bab, a bizzle will be soon.'

Madaflom rage was as bright as haze, big digly with higle truz.
A flyzoz had not done his waze, the calmness was just huz.

As a flyzoz, I want you to know about a Lisheng class.
A madaflom is a teacher and floors aren't made of grass.

Alex Brindle (12)
Redland Green School, Bristol

Why, Oh Why . . . ?

Even though I have a slight problem
And my back is a little bit curvy
It does not mean that I'm merely a toy
Or I'm too small to feel big and be loud.
Nor does it mean that I cannot have friends
Because in time it shall make amends.
Next year I shall have an operation
And tiny toy robot I shall be no more
For when it is all done and over,
I shall be strong and tall for the rest of my life.

Though after ten years I've grown used to my form,
This does not mean that I do not feel pain
From the words that have been thrown my way.
But when people stop to say 'Aaawwhh!' or sneer,
I shall simply walk away with no fear.

I ask myself: why, oh why can't people see me without my problem,
Just see me for who I am . . . ?

Saffy Haigh (12)
Redland Green School, Bristol

School Days

All of the hustle and bustle and rush,
Giggling girls gossiping about who is whose crush.

Everyone's rampaging, afraid to be late,
Except for the ball boy right next to the gate.

But nobody notices a shadow of a child,
Not afraid to be wrong, but afraid to be wild.

Unlike those who run havoc, start trouble, break rules,
Not everyone is like what you hear in schools.

I think that people should hear their friends' voices,
But don't hold back, try to make your own choices.

Jemima Pike (11)
Redland Green School, Bristol

Growing Up

I don't want to write this poem
Maybe it's my age.
Adults think it's fascinating,
Not just a scribbled page.

All I want is to be outside,
Soaking up the sun,
Or inside playing computer games,
With some friends, having fun!

But I'm just stuck here writing,
My life washing away.
Maybe soon I'll disappear,
I'm starting to decay.

Death lurks around the corner,
From *Bodmas,* books and bore;
School is hang, draw and quarter,
Growing up's a chore.

Helen Birch (11)
Redland Green School, Bristol

Can You See Me?

Can you see me in the corner crying?
Do you hate me or are you lying?
I can't do sports, does it really matter?
Peer-pressure mounting on me, am I getting taller?
People don't look at you, they smirk and turn
The criticism thrown at me, it scars, it burns
I thought going to a new school would make a change
They used to look at me, like an alien, so strange
What am I doing? Am I not giving?
Maybe I should just stop, just stop living.

Douglas Best (11)
Redland Green School, Bristol

Hope

Within the darkness, a speck of light will always live.
It offers its hand to the falling soldier,
He never takes, but always gives,
He eternally exists in the heart and memory of his mother,
The earth, the light, they are all one.

Where he falls . . . there, there will always be hope.
The clear long angel washes away all his troubles.
Then, runs back down to where she came from, leaving piles of rubble.
Peace, the sun, the fields and the flowers awake, with fire in their soul.

The Earth gives presents of morals, but also gives the protection of those who are loyal.
The soldier may be gone, but his soul is still treasured like gold.
Explosions and weapons may be fierce,
But . . . within the darkness, a speck of light will always live.

Basir Naz (13)
Redland Green School, Bristol

I Remember . . .

When I was six
And more grown up than five,
Toys and games I liked to fix
And in the pool I liked to dive.

When I was nine
But not yet ten,
I liked to go out to dine
Being ten is a good age to build a den.

I'm soon going to be twelve
But being eleven is still heaven.

Jake Jones (11)
St David's College, Llandudno

I Remember . . .

I remember the days
German bombers overhead,
Scrambling under my bed,
Listening to the sound,
Of the bombs exploding into the ground.

I remember
The family next door,
Having to move because of the war,
Move to the countryside,
I had to go too.

I remember
I was scared out of my wits,
Because of the Blitz.
I had no friends,
In this new house,
Except the mouse.

I remember
All who died
And so few survived,
This was the end,
The end of the war.

Nick Roden (12)
St David's College, Llandudno

Now I Am Twelve

When I was six I ate a Twix and wanted to fix
When I was seven it was Heaven.
When I was eight I lost some weight and started to hate.
When I was nine I had some wine and made a rhyme.
When I was ten I fed a hen.
When I was eleven I wanted to be seven.
Now I am twelve and it's alright.

Alexander Maguire (12)
St David's College, Llandudno

Girlfriends

When I was six
I met a girl
With dazzling eyes
And long blonde curls
No other girl compared to her
With her wonderful gaze.
I was in a daze.
She had me going for quite a while
With her wonderful ways
And incredible smile.
But then one day
She moved away
Without a word to me
And eventually
So did the memories,
But when I was twelve
I'd change a bit
And she came back
But she was still so dazzling
In every way.
I knew she really was the one.

Charlie Marshall (12)
St David's College, Llandudno

When I Was . . .

When I was six, I loved the colour pink.
But I didn't sleep a wink.
When I was six, I loved playing with dolls,
But I got scared when I read about trolls.
When I was six, I loved wearing party sandals,
But I could never reach door handles.

When I was nine, I loved the colour cream.
But I would wake up and tell my parents about my dream.
When I was nine, I loved playing the flute,
But I was scared when I heard an owl hoot.
When I was nine, I loved high heels,
But I never got on with my meals.

When I was twelve, I loved the colour red.
But I never wanted to go to bed.
When I was twelve, I loved playing with my dogs,
But I got scared when I saw a hog.
When I was twelve, I loved wearing long boots
But I fell over tree roots.

Zuzanna Kawalek (12)
St David's College, Llandudno

Growing Up

When I was six
I had my first Twix.

When I was seven
I moved to Devon.

When I was eight
I had my first date.

When I was nine
I thought life was fine.

When I was ten
I bought my first hen.

When I was eleven
I moved back from Devon.

Now I'm twelve
I'm doing English prep.

Douglas Seale (12)
St David's College, Llandudno

Growing Up

When I was six
I made a new best friend.

When I was seven
I dreamt of being eleven.

When I was eight,
I put on some weight.

When I was nine
I drank some wine.

When I was ten
I swallowed a pen.

When I was eleven
I was glad I was not seven.

Louie Forte (11)
St David's College, Llandudno

Aliens

Is there such a thing as a UFO?
Maybe this question we will never know.
Are there creatures from out of space?
Do they know of the human race?

Do these creatures just want to say hello?
Maybe yes? Maybe no?
Do they want to take our planet Earth?
Take it, for all its worth?

Do they abduct people into their ghostly ship?
Do they torture them with a frightening whip?
Are they angry with something we've done?
Are they trying to turn our thoughts on?

Is it true people see strange light
And run away, with a horrible fright?
Do people see flying things?
Are they round, do they have wings?

We will probably never know what is out there,
But will still see strange things.
But one day, we might find out,
What life in space is all about.

Joshua Ozanne (12)
St Sampson's High School, Guernsey

Recipe For A Perfect Piece Of Music

Begin with a bag full of lyrics,
Make sure they've been sprinkled on so tight.
Add a teaspoon of acoustic,
This will make the mixture have some melody.
Next stir in a beat in order to give it some heat.
Finally, add an ounce of tuneage otherwise it won't sound so great.
Bake for two or three minutes, so it's not too long or short.
Serve with a talented musician, just to top it all off.

Adele Le Gallez (14)
St Sampson's High School, Guernsey

Friends!

Friends are to laugh with,
Friends are for happiness,
We share secrets,
We care for each other,
We are there for each other.

Friends are to share things with,
We love each other,
We do everything together.
We have a good friendship,
We have sleepovers,
We sing, we laugh.

We will never separate,
We will never betray each other,
As we are all friends forever!

Louise Dorey (13)
St Sampson's High School, Guernsey

Recipe For The Perfect Friend!

Begin with bags full of trust
This will make the mixture with care.

Add a teaspoon of friendship
Add an ounce of fun!

Mix with loving
And add some always happy.

Next stir in with always got your back
Or always there for you
In order to help you!

Bake for ten minutes.

And serve with another bag of trust!

Ashleigh Pitman (14)
St Sampson's High School, Guernsey

The Perfect Holiday

Begin with bags full of sand

Add a teaspoon of beach chairs
And an ounce of the warm ocean.

Gently mix with very hot weather for added tan.

Next slowly stir in many palm trees in order to have
A nice shaded place to go.

Bake for five hours of paradise.

Then let it cool down with big ocean waves.

Finally, serve with handsome, good-looking lifeguards.

    Enjoy!

Laura Kirkpatrick (14)
St Sampson's High School, Guernsey

Name-Calling

Everyone hates being called names
We just wanna sit back or play games.

Being called Lame or a Nerd.
And they say they heard it from a little bird.

Just because we get highest in a test
It doesn't mean we're the best.

Everyone has the right to a good life
And not to have strife.

Leah Foss (12)
St Sampson's High School, Guernsey

A Recipe For A Perfect Teacher

Begin with a bag full of smiles
This will make the mixture soft and gentle.
Add a teaspoon of happiness
An ounce of effort.
Mix with enthusiasm,
For added taste a shovel of helpfulness.
Bake for two splendid minutes
Serve with delight and laughter.

Bethany Nicholson (11)
St Sampson's High School, Guernsey

The Man

80-year-old man looking up at the planes
Thinking of what happened in his days.
Just wondering when he will die
Or will he live or just fly?
What will happen to this man?
He wants to know what will happen.

Owen Hunt (12)
St Sampson's High School, Guernsey

Destiny

I know you can see me.
Even when I scream, scream, scream.
It's like I'm never there.
And when we finally meet, meet, meet
I'll show you around
Who are you to disagree?
This is my friend, Destiny.

Sonia Emerson (12)
Westlands School, Sittingbourne

War Has My Daddy

Once my daddy was here with my mum,
But now he's there, just a photo left,
As if all memory of him has gone,

With ash on his face and sand in his hair,
He walks on,
>Walks alone,
>>Walks with fear in his heart.

Like sharks to catch their fish,
They hide in the shadows,
They bite where it hurts,
Bang!
One more.

A breath of relief,
My daddy just called,
But he isn't coming home,
I remember the last time he tucked me in,
Whispered goodnight,
Softly kissed my head,
I wish I could have that last hug again,
Hold his warm hands,
Smile with him again,
I wish I could call him home,
Stop the war,
End it all.

I don't understand why they are fighting,
We would get told off at school,
But school isn't war,
War has my daddy,
Why won't they give my daddy back?

Georgina Jaggs (13)
Woking High School, Woking

Dear Diary

Do you promise
Not to read this out loud?
If you do
Then here we go . . .

How do I start?
Well, first he broke my heart
I like him
I thought he liked me.

He did at first
He started being mean
Saying he hated me
Was it true?

The next thing I know
He's over me
Asking out my best friends
One was true, one was to annoy me.

He thought it would get to me
But at the end of the day
After everything
It didn't.

I just thought he was . . .
Pathetic
Immature
And stupid.

He made me feel . . .
Worthless
Small
And angry.

Just when I thought nothing could get any worse
Someone who I thought was my friend
Obviously wasn't
How could she?

After all this time
That I had been letting out my feelings
For that stupid boy
To my 'friend'.

132

She asked him out
He said yes,
So much for a friend
So much for a boyfriend.

I now wish . . .
That I never . . .
Started with him . . .
From the start!

Now I know what it's like for
Someone to grab your heart
But then chuck it all back in your face!

Elvie Mathis (11)
Woking High School, Woking

The Beach

The waves roar in,
Swallows the cliffs.
Sand hot under feet.
Further down the beach,
The wet sand swallows feet.
Wind blows past,
Picking up sand,
Whip sand!
Sand hot under feet.
Further down the beach,
The wet sand swallows feet.
Surfboards zoom in,
To the core,
Carrying passengers,
Clothed in black.
Sand hot under feet.
Further down the beach,
The wet sand swallows feet.

Georgina Gray
Woking High School, Woking

Difficult Questions

'You must do this.
And you must do that.
Come over here!
Stand over there!'
I sit
I wonder.
Why?
Who makes the rules that say when the day ends?
Who decides who, what, where and when?
Where do our words come from?
Who made them up?
Who chooses Go and who chooses Stop?

Life is a riddle
And the world's like a game
The rules that we follow,
Make us all the same.

So then I ask you,
Why is there hate?
Why can't we love another?
Make the world a better place.

I know not the answers
But neither do you.
They're just some of those questions
So what can you do?

Lauren Brown (14)
Woking High School, Woking

Poem

Aliens from another planet
Come down in their spaceship
Hard and metal like a toy robot
Firing out fire
Hard, hot, killing.

Corey Aslin (14)
Woking High School, Woking

We All Love Cats!

Cats, cats, cats
They all love rats

Short cats, tall cats
Big cats, small cats
We all love cats

Fat cats, slim cats
Ugly cats, pretty cats
We all love cats

Happy cats, sad cats
Mad cats, boring cats
We all love cats

Spotty cats, stripy cats
Tabby cats, forest cats
We all love cats

Clean cats, smelly cats
Cool cats, posh cats
We all love cats

No matter what cat
You have, treat it
With respect and it
Will love you forever
In its own way.

Rebecca Brown (12)
Woking High School, Woking

That Second

That second I saw the thing exploding out of the water,
That second my heart was racing,
That second I saw its long sturdy tentacles and its fierce eyes,
That second I grabbed whatever I could,
That second I nearly died.

Ella Porter (14)
Woking High School, Woking

My Dog, Rocky

Small, mad and mental,
Three colours, brown, black and white,
As a puppy, he liked to bite,
Or maybe cause a fight,
Sleeps most of the day,
Whilst we're all away,
Playing is his nature,
Or nibbling on the furniture,
He loves to sleep,
In a big heap,
Jumps like a pogo stick,
Bouncing up and down,
If we shout,
He looks with a frown
As if to say, 'Pardon!'
We open the door
And off he goes
Running down the garden,
His small body and small tail
As cute as Noddy!
Now, that's my mad dog, Rocky!

Ashleigh Thatcher (12)
Woking High School, Woking

Aliens

Aliens, aliens, aliens,
Big, green, round,
Small, skinny, brown,
Walk, slither, slide,
Crawl, run, hide.

Aliens, aliens, aliens
Different types of aliens
They play, they fight, they fly,
All in the middle of the sky.

Emma Stone (14)
Woking High School, Woking

Christmas

Bright lights shine early morning
Glass like snowflakes fall from above
Pitter-patter of little feet running down the stairs
Screams of joy as children rip open presents
Rustles of paper flying on the floor
Lit up faces like light bulbs
Shimmering wrapping paper shiny as the sun
Louder screams as more presents arrive
Nan and Grandad with chocolate and sweets.
Finally quietness as breakfast comes out
Cereal, toast and jam of any flavour
Fresh orange juice splashing on pyjamas.
'Careful kids, calm down,' shouts Mum
They don't take any notice.
Cousins are here, means more presents have arrived
Clothes, jewellery, toys and sweets.
They are all such magical treats.
There are all different kinds of sweets today
Haribo, chocolate, lollies, hooray
Christmas is so much fun
I can't wait for another one!

Katie-Lauren Lewsza (11)
Woking High School, Woking

Volcano

Not long ago,
There was a big blow,
Volcanic ash came down,
Luckily not too near the ground,
Families were stranded,
No planes landed,
Planes were stuck,
We didn't have much luck,
It was a really big shock.

Chloe Alexis (12)
Woking High School, Woking

Deer Skin

Dappled in morning sunlight
Peaceful and alone
Grazing on dew-covered grass
Enjoying the silence
But then
Snap of a twig
Ears cocked, muscles tensed
Unnatural wind flowing just above my head
I bolt, I fly through the trees
They follow on light footsteps
More unnatural wind rippling the air
There is something in my leg
I panic and tumble
Slumping to the ground
My heart flies
Light and shallow
A shadow is over me
The shadow raises its arm
I am free . . .
Galloping through the flowers
In the bright sparkling meadow.

Isabel Meyler (12)
Woking High School, Woking

I'm The Toy In The Box That's Never Used

I'm the toy in the box that's never used
All the others are torn and abused,
My fur is old, but still new
And if I was a colour I'd be blue
'Cause I'll never be loved by you
I'm like a stone in your shoe
Never going to be loved by you
I have no idea what to do
So, I sit in the box waiting for you.

William Berry (12)
Woking High School, Woking

Torrents Of Darkness!

Torrents of darkness
They can be swallowed by a black love,
When two worlds collide
The worlds that collide are mostly different
But still possess the factor of freedom and
Honesty between each lover.

Torrents of darkness
Can be clamped shut stopping a perfect love being found
This would be the story of the one-sided love.
The handicapped hearts without the advantage of a free parking space.

Torrents of darkness
They are the gatemen of love letting and stopping desperation
Being met by a hand on a shoulder,
A light to brighten a heart or a desire to be with someone else.

Torrents of darkness
Are a form of love wishing and whirling
Into its own creative world
Leaving behind devastation in every victim's heart!

Sara Hill (12)
Woking High School, Woking

Rambo Fly

Guns, bombs, knives,
Slipping away the lives
Of enemies, big and small,
Stout, wide, short or tall.
Coming to the massive city,
To kill you all before you cry your pity.
The very big chance to die
Is certain in the arrival of the Rambo Fly!

Ayman Sinada (12)
Woking High School, Woking

Candyfloss

Candyfloss so sweet
Yet so sticky
With its yummy
Pink coat so
Soft like a sheep's.
Candyfloss so sweet,
So soft, so sticky
The candyfloss'
Smell flows through
The air and into
People's mouths.
Yummy,
Sticky,
Pink,
Fluffy,
Yummy,
Sticky,
Pink,
Fluffy,
Candyfloss.

Mia-Siân Worrall (12)
Woking High School, Woking

Untitled

If you were a leaf I'd give you a tree,
If you were a drop, I'd give you a sea,
If you were a planet, I'd give you a galaxy.

And if you were some honey I'd give you a bee,
If you were some sugar, I'd give you a strawberry,
If you were a kid, I'd give you a sweetie.

And if I were a leaf you'd give me a tree,
If I were a drop you'd give me a sea,
If I were a planet you'd give me a galaxy,
Gee, I'm glad it's not just me!

Vina Murad (12)
Woking High School, Woking

The War Is Done!

The arms of the crosses stretch for miles,
Sad families gather, with no smiles,
Tears roll down their broken faces
As they remember their hero.

The remaining soldiers come to show respect,
And it gives them a chance where they can reflect,
A dark grey cloud covers the sky,
And up there in Heaven are those who died.

The world sounds empty apart from the tears,
After loud guns for the last four years.
As the last few planes return home,
The bodies now lie there all alone.

The war is finally done,
And because of our soldiers, we have won,
We will never forget the sacrifice they gave
As we can now go and visit them at their grave.

Josh Bowden (13)
Woking High School, Woking

Poem On War

I work in the front line trenches,
Here in the middle of nowhere,
I've been begging to go home,
But I have courage to stay.

I pick up the bloodstained gun
With my shaking hand,
Dare I shoot,
Or will I just stare?

I'm, all alone,
No place to go,
Running and hiding
My heart stops.

Steph Hamill (13)
Woking High School, Woking

A Beautiful War

Why do we fight?
Why do we hate?
Why is pain
What we love to create?

The place that we live,
The place that we die,
Is the place that we love,
And the place we shall lie.

When young ones are led
To their early death,
When frightening war
Takes their beautiful breath.

The blood-red flowers
Are a symbol to us all
That peace and beauty is with
Everyone that falls.

Hannah Jones (13)
Woking High School, Woking

It's Not A Game

Remembering what happened - it scares me,
Flashbacks take control of my mind,
Squinting my eyes - trying not to see,
But it's no use - I have already seen it happen.

It was so quick it stopped me in my tracks,
A flash of silver plunged deep,
Looking back I could have helped,
But I ran away - not quick enough to see blood seep.

Once I got through the front door,
I collapsed - too full of shame,
This is my lesson, and this is what I've learnt,
Carrying a knife is not a game.

Megan Calderwood (13)
Woking High School, Woking

A Bad Driver

It was all over the newspapers,
Even on TV,
A man who went driving crazy,
It really scares me.

His car went fast as lightning,
Down the motorway,
He skipped all the traffic lights,
While shouting, 'Get out of my way!'

The sound of cars went *beep! Beep!*
The man's car grumbled with rage,
It skidded and screeched down the high street,
Like an animal in a cage.

Then the man lost control,
And there was a blinding flash,
The sound of screaming echoed,
As the man had a massive crash!

Valli McAdam (11)
Woking High School, Woking

Connor Is An Alien

Aliens are green
Aliens are ugly
Aliens are mean
Aliens are smelly.

Connor is green
Connor is ugly
Connor is mean
Connor is smelly.

Connor is an alien
Because they're both the same
Connor is an alien
Because they're both insane.

Jacob Parvin (14)
Woking High School, Woking

Abduction

My father was from Wales,
For life he herded sheep
An alien came down from space all day
And swept him off his feet.

He said, 'Hello' to the alien
They had a funny scent
He said, 'Hello' to the alien
They noticed his accent.

It turns out that Welsh people
Are a speciality on Mars
They took him to the slaughterhouse
It wasn't very far.

They served him with a woolly sheep
Some celery and bread
They put some gravy over him,
Shame that he was dead!

Jonathan Abraham (14)
Woking High School, Woking

Live A Lie

Can you be someone you're not?
Can you live a lie?
Can you lie to all the people,
But still feel alive?
Can you speak words that are not your own?
Can you throw away what you own?
And just live a lie?

Can you love the things you hate?
Can you hurt the ones you love?
Can you cover up your feelings?
Can you cover up the pain,
And just live a lie?

Sophie Osborne (12)
Woking High School, Woking

Liberal Democrats

L abour's enemies
I n the winning
B eat the rest
E very winner
R unning the country is what we do best
A waiting for answers
L ate to be known

D efeating the rest did not happen
E vacuating us from the table
M atters are important
O ver the moon
C onservatives' enemies
R ates are down
A t the edge
T he ending came
S o that's for us.

Jordon Hattersley (12)
Woking High School, Woking

The Beginning Of The End

They come in their numbers
They come in the night

They caused all this madness
They caused all this fright

They came to this planet
They came to this state

They killed all those people
They created this hate

Our weapons are useless
Our tactics are fly

We must get away
Or we will all die.

David Dennington (13)
Woking High School, Woking

My Poem

I listen to my heartbeat in my seat
Wondering when it's next going to beat
Then I think to myself when I grow older
That I used to have a good time pretending to be a soldier,
I had a good time when I was younger.

I listen to my heartbeat in my seat
Whilst I'm waiting for a little treat
Nobody knows what it is
But it makes me go all dizz.

I listen to my heartbeat
In my seat
Five past four on the dot
In a classroom
On a seat
Listening to my heart beat, beat, beat.

Corinne Heggie (14)
Woking High School, Woking

The Election 2010

The election coming up,
David Cameron, Gordon Brown, Nick Clegg,
Conservatives, Labour, Liberal Democrats,
Hearts beating like a drum,
Who will win?
Hearts beating like ongoing footsteps,
'I must win!'
They all say,
'I'm the best, trust me,'
They all say,
But only one of the enemies can win,
'He's rubbish,'
'He's an idiot,'
The same thing from all of them,
Who will win?

Christopher Shah (12)
Woking High School, Woking

The Eruption

It happened three weeks ago
On a terrible darkened day
When a great explosion was heard all over and
A thick cloud fell over Iceland like a big, thick blanket.
The dust clogged every crack
And the lava scorched everything in its path
Like an army tank killing in war.

People were stuck in unfamiliar countries
And there was nothing they could do.
The ash spread for miles all over the world
And put dust on innocent things.

People struggled to breathe fresh air
Like someone drowning, trying desperately to get to the surface.
It killed many people and injured many more
All because of one eruption.

Phoebe Stanmore (12)
Woking High School, Woking

Everyone Hates Poetry

I hate poetry,
There is no point,
What is it meant to do?
I hate poetry
Like every living thing.

Aliens hate poetry
They did not travel thousands of light years
To hear some rhyming slang.
Aliens hate poetry,
Like every living thing.

Poetry is like setting your head on fire
It is pointless and painful.
I'd rather set my head on fire
Than read poetry.

Connor Mitchell (14)
Woking High School, Woking

Jamie Is The Best

J oyful
A ccurate
M oney grabber
I mmoderate
E motional

I mpatient
S pendthrift

T earaway
H elpless
E ncouraging

B lithe
E nchanting
S illy
T riathlete.

Jamie Banszky (12)
Woking High School, Woking

Shopping

I walk on the shiny marble floor
I look around and I see clothes, accessories, bags and shoes
My heels are ticking like a clock.

I walk into a shop and I say
'Oh my gosh!' I look near the window
And I see a bright pink frock!

'Stunning, fabulous,' I say
In fact I could stay here all day
Loving these shops I just can't stay way.

Look on my right, down comes my purse,
Open it up and no papers.
A tear drips out of my eye
I walk out of the shop with shame.
Well all I can do now is tell Daddy to give me an extra claim.

Maryam Hussain (13)
Woking High School, Woking

The Murder

As I was watching the TV,
All over the news was nothing but me!
With a sudden rush of guilt inside,
I went to my room to curl up and hide.

I can't believe I did it,
It happened so very fast
I just grabbed a broken vase,
And she came up behind me,
'Darling, I'm off to work,' and bang!
She was dead.

So here I am now
Locked behind bars
I really don't know how,
But it went so fast.

Jennifer Kirk (11)
Woking High School, Woking

A Speck Of Hope

There's always hope,
Even in the mist of war.
In the darkest hour,
People forget,
Of a speck.
The speck that saves,
The speck that helps
The speck that warms,
People's doubts.
There's always hope,
Even in the mist of war.
The hope of a speck,
The speck of hope,
The speck that is always warm.

Daniel Pearce (11)
Woking High School, Woking

Bacon

This poem is not suitable for vegetarians.

Bacon is nice
But some people think it is wrong
So I have made up a song

I smell bacon, I smell pork,
I smell piggy on the end of my fork.

So I think that bacon is sweet
Such very nice meat
What a treat
I can't think of any more words that rhyme
So I will stop this poem in this moment of time.

Finley Sale (12)
Woking High School, Woking

Animals

We trap them in cages,
We set them free,
We say, 'They don't matter.'
We feed them our food,
We take care of them.
We take them to the vet's,
We say, 'They are like maniacs.'
We say we can help them.
Animals are people.
Animals deserve better.
We say they need us
But are you sure they really do?

Sophie Little (12)
Woking High School, Woking

Gone

She was walking along the road,
All alone,
At night.
She had no idea what was coming.
If only she'd looked,
It was right there.
It came quietly,
Being sneaky,
Being scary.
Bang!
She was gone,
Dead.

Jennie Bew (12)
Woking High School, Woking

Dream Time

Dreaming . . .
It's a virtual world,
Speeding in my car,
I jump into my bed,
Pop on my virtual reality helmet,
Zooming through the countryside,
With my sidekick by my side,
Driving to town,
Wearing my gown,
I hop out of my car . . .
It falls down!
Nightmare!

Raheem Yusif Hussain (12)
Woking High School, Woking

Unknown Conflict

We watch the stars and other planets
But do they watch us back?

Do they know of our existence
Or like us do they remain in darkness?

Are they merely curious
Or do they want something, us?

If we met another life,
Would our planet erupt in flames?

Or will we be the predator
And cause their destruction?

Nazmiye Raif (14)
Woking High School, Woking

The Volcano

An airport with more people than there has ever been
'All planes grounded' is one of the things you hear on TV.
People begging the staff to let them go home
There's a volcano. It erupted.
But people are just thinking about them.
They don't care about the people who have to live there
Through the pain and the hurt.
I do though. I care about them.
Because I'm there watching it happen.
My family and friends staggering like a twig in a fire.
And no one cares.

Daisy Jones (11)
Woking High School, Woking

World Cup

Do you ever think the World Cup is a fix?
England won it in 1966,
And on that year of celebration
They just so happened to be the home nation,
1930 was the year of the World Cup's inauguration,
Uruguay won the first World Cup,
Along with the ref's pet pup,
Italy won in 1934,
And the hosting nation wins the World Cup once more,
So here's a plan if all else fails,
Make sure the next one takes place in Wales.

Jordan Hookins (12)
Woking High School, Woking

Paint

I sit there for hours with my paintbrush
My piece of paper is like a long, glowing field
I glide, slide and slip around the page
My hands are covered in paint
I imagine everything in such little time
After a while I am able to picture it
Colours everywhere
Paints.

Elizabeth Nay (14)
Woking High School, Woking

Untitled

Fighting in what looks like a nightmare
Where every second you have to be aware
Boom, crash, shells and guns are all I can hear,
Heat, boiling sun is all I can feel
That and a wound in my shoulder.

Nadeem Hussain
Woking High School, Woking

Fish

Swimming in the ocean, bobbing up and down,
Making bubbles as he breathes. Nibbling on floating seaweed
Enjoying the company of nearby crabs.
Swimming in the ocean, with the freedom to float.
Seeing the shadows of nearby boats.
Peeping up to see the dry land,
Seeing the glimmering of the shining sand.
For I am a fish and I like to float, swim, bob and gloat.

Abigail Hookins (12)
Woking High School, Woking

Election

E lections
L et
E veryone
C hoose
T o
I ndividually
O ppose
N ew prime ministers.

Megan MacAlister (12)
Woking High School, Woking

2010 Election

The election's coming up
David Cameron, Gordon Brown or Nick Clegg
They're all fighting to be PM of England
Labour, Conservative or Liberal Democrats
Who's going to win?
No one knows
Who do you want to win?
It's down to you.

Lewis Sines (11)
Woking High School, Woking

9/11

It's been a year now, Daddy
I really, really miss you.
We had your favourite dinner tonight,
I ate it all up.
Mum says I have to go to bed now.
I sleep with the light on,
Just in case you come back and kiss me goodnight.

Chloe Marsh (14)
Woking High School, Woking

So Much

So much depends upon . . .
The white clock
The hands are going in a big circle
To show the time.

Ben Hooper (14)
Woking High School, Woking

Hearts

Hearts
As fragile as glass
Snap, crack, break
Heartbroken.

Alice Curr
Woking High School, Woking

Blue

Ocean
As big as the sky
Soft, calm, powerful
Ocean.

Ayesha Rasool (14)
Woking High School, Woking

War Poem

Guns
As dangerous as an animal
Bang, boom, ouch
On the floor, destroyed.

Idrees Ifzal (14)
Woking High School, Woking

The White Snowman

So much depends upon the white snowman
Melting from the sunlight,
Waiting to be built again!

Gemma Hemus (14)
Woking High School, Woking

Past Poets - Future Voices Expressions From The UK

Young Writers Information

We hope you have enjoyed reading this book - and that you will continue to enjoy it in the coming years.

If you like reading and writing poetry drop us a line, or give us a call, and we'll send you a free information pack.

Alternatively if you would like to order further copies of this book or any of our other titles, then please give us a call or log onto our website at www.youngwriters.co.uk.

Young Writers Information
Remus House
Coltsfoot Drive
Peterborough
PE2 9JX
(01733) 890066